No
Straight
Road
Takes You
There

Also by Rebecca Solnit from Granta Books

Wanderlust: A History of Walking

River of Shadows: Eadweard Muybridge and the Technological Wild West

A Paradise Built in Hell: The Extraordinary Communities That Arise in Disaster

The Faraway Nearby

Men Explain Things to Me: And Other Essays

The Mother of All Questions: Further Feminisms

Call Them by Their True Names: American Crises (and Essays)

Whose Story is This? Old Conflicts, New Chapters

Recollections of My Non-Existence

Orwell's Roses

No Straight Road Takes You There

Essays for Uneven Terrain

Rebecca Solnit

GRANTA

Granta Publications, 12 Addison Avenue, London W11 4QR

First published in Great Britain by Granta Books, 2025

Copyright © 2025 Rebecca Solnit

This book was first published in the United States by Haymarket Books, Chicago, in 2025, with the generous support of Lannan Foundation, Wallace Action Fund, and Marguerite Casey Foundation.

The right of Rebecca Solnit to be identified as the author of this work has been asserted by her in accordance with the Copyright, Designs and Patents Act, 1988.

All rights reserved. This book is copyright material and must not be copied, reproduced, transferred, distributed, leased, licensed or publicly performed or used in any way except as specifically permitted in writing by the publisher, as allowed under the terms and conditions under which it was purchased or as strictly permitted by applicable copyright law. Any unauthorized distribution or use of this text may be a direct infringement of the author's and publisher's rights, and those responsible may be liable in law accordingly.

A CIP catalogue record for this book is available from the British Library.

10 9 8 7 6 5 4

ISBN 978 1 80351 164 1
eISBN 978 1 80351 166 5

Offset by Iram Allam
Printed and bound by CPI Group (UK) Ltd, Croydon, CR0 4YY

The manufacturer's authorised representative in the EU
for product safety is Authorised Rep Compliance Ltd,
71 Lower Baggot Street, Dublin D02 P593 Ireland
(arccompliance.com)

www.granta.com

Contents

In Praise of the Indirect, the Unpredictable, the Immeasurable, the Slow, and the Subtle	1

VISIONS

A Truce with the Trees	11
Sky Full of Forests	18
On Letting Go of Certainty in a Story That Never Ends	24
Tortoise at the Mayfly Party	33
In Praise of the Meander	39
Insurrectionary Aunthood	45

REVISIONS

Despair Is a Luxury	65
On Not Meeting Nazis Halfway	75
Against Centrism and Its Biases	82
In the Shadow of Silicon Valley	88
Masculinity as Radical Selfishness	104
Abortion Is an Economic Issue	110
Toward a Democracy of Voices	116
The Storykiller and His Sentence	121
Feminism Has Just Begun	126

MORE VISIONS

Deep Time Versus Short Term	135
Changing the Climate Story	141
Climate of Abundance	155
The Great Transformation	161
Hope on Far Horizons	165

Credo	170
Acknowledgments	172
Publication Credits	175

In Praise of the Indirect, the Unpredictable, the Immeasurable, the Slow, and the Subtle

How we see the world has everything to do with what we can do in the world. Action is shaped by vision—the frameworks through which we understand the world—or so it has long seemed to me. This is why, in my writing of the past few decades, I've tried to offer not just my views but what I hope can serve as equipment for anyone considering history, power, change, and possibility. This anthology is made up of essays aspiring to do exactly that, and as I gathered them I realized how much my own credo—or arsenal—is made up of celebrations of indirection.

It's not that I have anything against the easy, the immediate, the obvious, the straightforward, and the predictable. It's just that I think much of what we face and endeavor to achieve requires an embrace or at least a recognition of its opposite. So I have chased after the long trajectories of change as both the often forgotten events and ideas leading up to a rupture, a breakthrough, or a revolution, and the often overlooked indirect consequences that come afterward. I've celebrated how a movement that may not achieve its official goal may nevertheless generate or inspire those indirect consequences that matter sometimes as much or more than the original goal. I've also noticed how often a movement is dismissed as having failed during the slow march to victory, when victory comes.

As for victory, I am all for what Jules Lobel of the Center for Constitutional Rights calls "success without victory": lawsuits that lost in court but nevertheless advanced their issues as part of larger human-rights campaigns. I've become a lover of slowness, patience, endurance, and long-term vision, because these things seem like crucial equipment for changing the world or even understanding it. And I've become a storyteller who seeks out examples of these tools at work, as I've come to recognize that changing the story, dismantling the stories that trap us, finding stories adequate to our realities, are foundational to finding our powers and possibilities.

Too, I find beauty in complexity. In tracing the drawn-out paths of influence. In seeing the intricate webs of relationship and causality. In witnessing the powers of stubborn patience and and long-term vision. In recognizing how often change begins in the periphery, with movements and thinkers once dismissed as insignificant, even though as it progresses it often moves toward the center to complete its journey in the spotlights shining on the centers of power. In knowing how much culture—which I think of as operating in the deep substrata of our collective worldviews—shapes the surface levels on which politics play out. In embracing the truth that, though we may not know how and why something might matter when we do it, it may nevertheless matter immensely (and how the measure of its value may be impossible to assess for decades or lifetimes after it happens, because sometimes a book or an act or an idea is a gift bequeathed to a posterity the giver could

In Praise of the Indirect, the Unpredictable, the Immeasurable 3

not imagine). In valuing the small events—coincidences, meetings, epiphanies—that often lead to large impacts. The terms *shortsighted* and *inevitable* are familiar; I would love to have *longsighted* as a term for the capacity to see patterns unfold over time, and maybe *evitable* as the opposite of *inevitable*.

Speaking of evitability, I've cherished unpredictability as the other face of possibility—if you already know what's going to happen, there's nothing more or nothing else possible, a view that often leads to disengagement and passivity. But mostly we don't know; those proclamations about inevitability are often false prophesies. Hope in this sense is just the recognition that in that uncertainty there may be the space in which to move toward the best and away from the worst of those possibilities, that the future is not (as it is so often spoken of) a place that already exists, toward which we are trudging, but a place that we are creating with what we do and how we do it (or don't) in the present. Or, rather, hope is that recognition and a commitment to the pursuit of the better possibilities within the spaciousness of the unknown, the not yet created. As Audre Lorde said, "To refuse to participate in the shaping of our future is to give it up. Do not be misled into passivity either by false security (*they don't mean me*) or by despair (*there's nothing we can do*). Each of us must find our work and do it."

But discomfort with uncertainty manifests as fatalism, pessimism, doomerism, despair—or sometimes as optimism—when it pretends that we know for certain what will happen. It reduces the vastness of the unknown into the known, the false certainty that pretends to know as a means of ignoring the fact that we don't. The likely happens often, but the unlikely happens often enough that it cannot be disregarded. The things that seem obvious, predictable, inevitable in hindsight were often regarded beforehand as impossible or unlikely, and an accurate memory of that equips us to aspire again to what we're told cannot happen. The misremembering of the past (or not remembering the past at all) ill equips us to face the future.

Memory is a power, especially memory that can perceive the larger patterns, the longer shifts, just as forgetting and amnesia are vulnerabilities. Intergenerational conversations, knowledge of history, and the habit of seeking context all contribute to that power. As the preeminent historian of the possible, Howard Zinn, put it: "There is a tendency to think that what we see in the present moment will continue. We forget how often we have been astonished by the sudden crumbling of institutions, by extraordinary changes in people's thoughts, by unexpected eruptions of rebellion against tyrannies, by the quick collapse of systems of power that seemed invincible. What leaps out from the history of the past hundred years is its utter unpredictability." I've tried to find other ways of seeing and to prize the migratory routes ideas take; the way that hope is most often grounded in memory, because you can't see the future, but you can understand the patterns and possibilities if you know the past.

At this point in my life, I have lived through social, political, and scientific changes that would have been not just unbelievable but in many cases inconceivable in my youth, and I know more about such change as a student of history. We all live in a world wilder than was dreamed of by almost any science-fiction version of it (fewer jetpacks but more gender-bending, less space travel but more space for other versions of how to be human, of who and what matter). I've come to share Zinn's perspective that, though the future is uncertain, the past provides insight—both in how ordinary people have mounted campaigns to change the world and how often that change has been unpredictable. The modest-looking movements that ultimately toppled the authoritarian regimes of Eastern Europe in 1989 surprised even their participants. The resurgence in power and visibility of indigenous peoples of the Americas, in this millennium, including widespread recognition of their rights and the value of their worldviews, was not foreseen in the last. That we are beneficiaries of movements from decades before, and that those movements would transform as their understanding evolved, are reminders of the ongoing process and that we are always in one way or another in the middle of the story.

The discomfort with temporal uncertainty that manifests as false certainty about the future has, I've come to realize, an equivalent in the unease about ambiguity, complexity, contradiction, and opacity that manifests as the urge to stuff reality into airtight categories. Categories are inevitable—language itself is a collection of categories—but their leakiness and limits should be recognized. Sometimes comparing something to something else or labeling it clarifies its essential nature. Sometimes it obscures it, because the differences matter or because that essential nature is heterogenous or altogether unclear.

Categories too often become where thought goes to die. That is, there's a widespread tendency to act as if once something has been categorized, no further consideration is required. But, often, it is. There are few terms I've reverted to more frequently than one the Utah-based environmental writer Chip Ward long ago uttered in my hearing. His "tyranny of the quantifiable" recognizes that often the impact and value of a person, a work of art, an action, a movement, a place, a system is not going to fit into the categories or be measurable by the usual yardsticks.

We are forever confronted with complexities, contradictions, ambiguities, with bad people doing something good or/and good people doing something terrible, and, more than any of these, with the fact that so often we don't know. Most of the time, we don't fully know who someone is, where they come from, what's going on with them in the present that may impact their ability to show up, how they may have changed so that their view from years ago is not their view now, how they may have been misrepresented. (We are not infrequently mysteries even to ourselves.) I value giving the benefit of the doubt to that which is not absolutely certain, a general-purpose equivalent to the legal concept of innocent until proven guilty. Social media has turned too many who use it into would-be pundits and false prophets by encouraging summary judgments and opinions not grounded in facts and expertise. People seem to feel naked, in these circumstances without an opinion, and dress themselves up in anything that comes to hand, especially what everyone else around them seems to be wearing. Knowing we don't know is an important form of knowledge and even wisdom that should never be replaced by the illusion of knowledge—but often is.

In this book, in essays both for (mostly gathered under the heading "Visions") and against (in the section called "Revisions"), I've tried to map the circuitous routes that change takes, the byways and backroads by which movements have been built and ideas have advanced, the times when no path forward exists—but, as the poet Antonio Machado famously said, "Walker, there is no path; the path is made by walking." For so many of our destinations, no straight road takes us there. The route is over mountains or through forests and beyond what we know—and it may also be through inconceivable beauty and transformation as well as peril; it may be uncharted, or steep, or take decades or centuries to traverse; we may get there through storytelling, alliance, or the appearance of some unanticipated participants. That's a declaration of difficulty and uncertainty but also of possibility that I offer as encouragement to keep going.

Note: All the following essays were written over the past few years, often in response to specific circumstances—the early days of the pandemic, the criminal conviction of a rapist, the aftermath of the 2020 election. I've chosen essays I think have something to say beyond the moment, and I've indicated the specifics of that moment when relevant.

I.
Visions

A Truce with the Trees

For the last fifty years, David Harrington, the founder and artistic director of San Francisco's Kronos Quartet, has been playing what he calls "pretty athletic music" on a violin made in 1721. I've heard him play all kinds of compositions on it, from the galloping notes of "Orange Blossom Special" to the minimalism of Terry Riley and even the occasional bit of Bach. The instrument, made by Carlo Giuseppe Testore in Milan, has survived three centuries, providing music for countless audiences, and can be heard on more than sixty Kronos albums.

When I first learned the age of the instrument, I was filled with wonder that a delicate piece of craftsmanship could endure for centuries, that something so small and light could do so much, that an instrument made in the eighteenth century could have so much to say in the twenty-first. It felt like a messenger from the past and an emblem of the possible, both a relic and a promise.

This violin is from before. Before James Watt invented the steam engine, which became a voracious, ubiquitous device, devouring coal and wood, then oil; driving mills, looms, pumps, then locomotive and steamboat engines. Before we began gouging out the Earth frantically to feed those steam engines and then those internal combustion engines. Before we dug out so much of the carbon that plants had so beautifully sequestered deep in the Earth eons ago. Before human impact exploded into a destructive force with the power to change the acidity of the oceans and the content of the atmosphere.

The sheer thrift of an instrument that lasted so long said to me that maybe you could have magnificent culture with material modesty, that the world before all our fossil fuel extraction and burning could be plenty elegant, and maybe that the world we need to make in response to climate change can feel like one of abundance, not austerity.

But fossil fuels have been poisonous, literally and politically. Renouncing them in an age when renewables have become better—as in cleaner, cheaper, more universally available—sources of power means giving up something that has contaminated our world and impoverished our confidence in the future. We tend to think of abundance as material stuff, but perhaps our piles of loot overshadow less tangible things that also matter, including continuity with the past, confidence in the future, and the cultural richness that is not just a commodity.

Harrington's violin is clearly a working instrument: a little battered, with a worn finish, a lot of tiny nicks and a visible crack. Its materials are themselves a sort of global gathering, all of the original ones organic and not involving mining, although metal tools would have been crucial to making the instrument. A violin is usually made of spruce wood on the front, or belly, and of maple on the back, sides, and neck. Traditionally, a violin's fingerboard and tailpiece were made of ebony from south Asia or Africa, though because it's now an endangered tree, contemporary instrument makers mostly use other wood (outside of China, where considerable ebony is still used).

The glue that holds the instrument together would have been made from boiling animal hides, and the varnish might have included shellac, made from a secretion of the south Asian lac insect, or just pine sap and some kind of vegetable oil, often linseed oil from flax. The strings were once made of sheep gut (not catgut, popular though the term is), though these days they tend to be metal and synthetic materials. Rosin, made from tree resin and rubbed on the horsehair of the bow, allows for the bow to sound on the strings—without it, Harrington notes, the instrument would be silent. When I was an unpromising child violinist, the clear amber lump of rosin was one of my favorite things about playing the instrument.

Nearly all bows are still strung with horsehair. Because mares tend to urinate on their tails, the ideal material is the white hair of the tail of a stallion or gelding, usually from Siberia, Mongolia, Canada, or Argentina. A few years ago, a bow maker told Harrington that, because of the climate crisis, it was harder to get the strong horsehair cold climates produce. For centuries, violin bows were made, by preference, from pernambuco wood from Brazil's Atlantic forests, specifically from the heartwood, the dense rings of orange-brown wood at the center of the tree. These trees are likewise endangered and avoided by many instrument makers now. Bow makers and violin makers have joined conservationists to form the International Pernambuco Conservation Initiative to protect and regenerate the species and the forests in which the trees grow.

One bow could bring together the Arctic and the tropics, and, if it was inset with ivory, abalone, or mother of pearl, as many are, also incorporate materials from the ocean or another continent. A violin with ebony and ivory and a pernambuco bow is a relic of the colonialism in which Europe enriched itself with materials from other continents, but it is also an all-renewable-materials artifact.

Mostly, a violin is trees. The spruce and maple with which violins are made also face impacts from climate change. You can see the spruce tree rings on the front of David's violin as a series of fairly even lines of growth—but erratic weather produces erratic rings, and the spruces used for Italian violins grow in the Dolomites, and the climate there is shifting. In those mountains is a famous forest known as "the forest of violins," because so many instruments were made for so long with its wood. As the climate continues to change, this place may cease to be the ideal source of wood for instruments, and increasingly erratic weather worldwide could make consistent wood grain rarer, too.

Violin maker and scholar Nancy Benning says that woods used by Stradivari, the legendary luthier whose life straddled the seventeenth and eighteenth centuries, and his peers had a climate element to them:

> Decades of colder temperatures in Italy, Switzerland, and Germany led to slower growth of the spruce trees. In particular, the woods used in Cremonese violins are believed to have superior tonal expressiveness and projection, thanks to the density (that is, the tightness of the tree rings) of the cold-grown spruce trees. It's the wood's vibrational efficacy and the effective production of sound that distinguish this rare and highly valued family of violins from others.

According to a report in *Nature Climate Change*, Norway spruces in central Europe now grow a third to three-quarters faster than they once did. Perhaps there will be Anthropocene instruments with their own sounds, from trees whose voices have changed with the climate. My violin-maker friend, Hans Johannson, is grounded in the great tradition but facing the future with interest rather than fear. "I'm not afraid of things changing, and I don't think magic is going to disappear," he told me a few years ago. Based in Reykjavik, he brews his own hide glue and varnishes and makes instruments with hand tools, much as Stradivari and Testore would have. His instruments are played in orchestras and quartets around the world, but he has also made experimental instruments and tested new materials.

Though computers can help, the craft still relies on the ear as well as the hand. Hans notes that "one of the reasons for the difficulty of mass producing violins is the fact that the wood never has the same properties, even pieces of spruce or maple from the same tree. When the flitches of wood are held and struck with a blow of the fist, some pieces are found to vibrate loudly with a long ringing tone, whereas other pieces sound dull and the note dies away quickly." It is conceivable that the cellos and violins he's made will be played as long as the Testore violin used by Harrington has been; that in the year 2322, someone will be playing a Johannson instrument.

Like all plants, all forests, the trees from which the Testore violin was made had been pulling carbon dioxide out of the atmosphere and sequestering it in their wood and in the Earth. The fossil fuel we burn now is an end product of carbon sequestered by plants eons ago. The violin is a tiny carbon sink, a reserve of carbon that didn't go back into the air but stayed here and sang.

I often think of what we are doing with our frenetic burning of fossil fuels as a sort of war against the trees. It's how we put back in the atmosphere the carbon they pulled out of it and continue to pull out of it—forests across the Earth are said to sequester about a quarter of the carbon we put into the atmosphere annually. The other three members of Kronos[*] also play instruments that hail from other eras. John Sherba's violin was made in New York in

---

[*] In the time since I wrote this essay, these three members of Kronos have moved on, and other musicians have joined the quartet.

1884, when atmospheric carbon was at 293 parts per million, only 16 points higher than in 1721. It was crafted the year before Carl Benz in Germany made the first petroleum-powered automobile. Sunny Yang's cello was made in Italy in 1903, when the reading was 296.8 parts per million, the same year the first Model A Ford was sold, and the Wright brothers flew the world's first successful heavier-than-air powered aircraft. Hank Dutt's viola was made in Italy in 1913, three years after we crossed the threshold of 300 parts per million, the year the Model T became the first truly mass-produced automobile.

These instruments come from a world in which petroleum-based plastic was just emerging, the great tropical forests were largely intact, and the seasonal cycles had not been disrupted, but also from a world in which Africa was largely ruled by European powers and many human rights had hardly been conceived of, let alone realized anywhere on Earth. The past tells many stories and always points to one story—that change is constant, for the better, for the worse.

One evening not long ago, I went to see the San Francisco Symphony's annual concert with the Oakland Interfaith Gospel Choir. The symphony musicians sat in a semicircle that began with violins and violas and ended with cellos and basses, and, thanks to the time I'd spent contemplating David Harrington's violin, I saw it as a forest of wooden instruments. The gospel singers stood above them, and at one moment, when I could see dozens of bows moving in unison in the dimness, see fifty mouths open in song, it felt like some kind of truce between our species and the trees had been struck.

Maybe that's the promise David's violin seemed to hold when I discovered how long it had been playing. At my request, he brought it over to my apartment and took it out of its case. I was a bit overawed and ready to spread a clean cloth to lay it on, but he put it on my table without any fuss and let me pick it up. It felt like a bird when I held it: almost weightless, incredibly powerful, and extremely delicate. And then I saw Kronos perform one more time, and there it was, in David's hands, making music as it had for three centuries, seeming strong enough to go on indefinitely.

Sky Full of Forests

Two figures on the beach, everybody and nobody, looking outward in an era when we might wonder what trouble they look out on. These days, these days of intense climate disruption, trouble can be anywhere. Are they looking at an ominous sky with unusual weather, a rising sea, a failing fishery, a ship to come from over the horizon? Are they taking refuge on the coast from inland fires, as people near me did in the 2017 fires in Sonoma County, California, or seeking refuge from a heat wave by the ocean that has soaked up so much of the excess heat in recent decades and still gives off coolness in warm places? Are they looking at the natural world—by which we mean the totality of the Earth systems within which the human has always been contained—for comfort or in watchful anxiety and apprehension? Do they see reassurance or uncertainty? What do they see?

What is refuge and what is peril are questions we can ask for each and all of us about each place and all of them.

I think of a summer Sunday morning of my own not long ago.

This essay was written in response to the photograph described here of two women on a coastline and was first published as the afterword to the anthology *Harvest Moon: Poems and Stories from the Edge of the Climate Crisis*, published in 2021 by the Philippines-based Institute for Climate and Sustainable Cities.

The sky was full of forests.

Full of faraway forests, the carbon they had drawn out of the air put back by fire so that the air was full of ash and particles, the wildfire smoke serving as a horribly familiar filter, making the sun red, the moon orange, the sky gray, the air harmful to breathe, the light wrong—golden but pallid, as if from some star other than our familiar sun. I had gone a thousand miles from home, but home had followed me as these ghost forests burning in California's mountains. I had intended to take the long way home and visit friends on the way, but, instead, I took the other, smoke-free route, because I could not bring myself to plunge deeper into the stinging smoke. I had spent too many weeks in that smoke in the burning years of 2017, 2018, 2019, and 2020.

Many years before, a Zen Buddhist priest in Lower Manhattan, Enkyo Pat O'Hara, had told me of the days after 9/11, when the rubble that had been the World Trade Center Towers was smoldering, "You had the sense that you were breathing people. It was like the smell of gunpowder or the smell of explosion. It was the smell of all kinds of things that had totally disintegrated, including people. People and electrical things and stone and glass and everything."

Now we were breathing forests.

It was the fifth year of the great fires in California, fires that ate tens of thousands of square kilometers of forests, ate towns and villages, ate birds and mammals, human and wild and domestic, ate the homes of people I knew, fires that broke all records, fires that made their own weather, fires that filled the air with clouds of smoke that photographers documented blowing over the Kansas prairie and Great Lakes, smoke that reached New York City, smoke that said everything is connected, is a nightmare, is a dream.

As I write, I hear on the radio that smoke inhalation by pregnant women leads to premature births: what's up in the heavens reaches all the way down within us to the very youngest.

As North America's Western sky filled with smoke in what has become a dread annual event, two months' rain fell in a few days on Germany, washing away buildings that had stood for centuries, because they had never stood under skies like these before. Flooding in the Chinese city of Zhengzhou proceeded so rapidly it drowned subway passengers; flooding in Lagos, Nigeria, was becoming chronic; flash floods in the Congo and Uganda were also taking place; and drought-furthered fires were raging in Greece and Turkey. When it came to water, we were entering an era of too much and not enough, thirsty wildlife and farms, reservoirs dry as desert bones, seawater lapping at South Pacific islands, glacier melt in Nepal, an ice storm in Texas. Of too much, not enough, and water arriving with a force that hit us like violence. We are leaving behind our old familiar world whose stability we can remember as a great kindness and entering into a rough new set of circumstances.

Like refugees leaving a place, we are leaving a time. What should we carry with us?

You could make an atlas of trouble out of floods and droughts and fires and famines, out of the instability of what we counted on for our stability and our sustenance in body and spirit and hope. One of the questions that arises for me is what will sustain us through this period. We will need stories more than ever. Those of us alive in this time, at least those of us who were lucky enough to live through some of the stable years and maybe the comparatively stable twentieth century for a few or several decades, must become holders of the baselines, and future generations must pick up these stories when we lay them down, our journeys done.

If we don't remember how things were, we cannot endeavor to restore what has been broken, and we cannot know why it is worth doing all the things that the latest IPCC report assures us can roll some of this back. This was the passage that told us so:

> Deliberate removal of carbon dioxide (CO_2) from the atmosphere could reverse … some aspects of climate change. However, this will only happen … if deliberate removals are larger than emissions. Some climate change trends, such as the increase in global surface temperature, would start to reverse within a few years. Other aspects … would take decades (e.g., permafrost thawing) or centuries (e.g., acidification of the deep ocean) to reverse, and some, such as sea level rise, would take centuries to millennia to change direction.

Enslaved people pursuing freedom in the United States navigated by the Big Dipper, the great constellation visible in the northernmost sky of the Northern Hemisphere, pointing to the North Star. We must have landmarks and dreams ahead of us to orient ourselves, to remember that it has been different and could be different. We must have a vision of what our toil is for and how we will know when we get there.

I fear something I often see in my own amnesiac country, the acceptance of what should be unacceptable, the mistaking for inevitable or eternal those destructive things that are neither.

That is, I fear forgetting.

Memory of how we slipped into trouble and misery and what came before can help us journey out of it. We must remember. Not to be nostalgic, but to know that there is something better than chaos and decline. In my country, in which intergenerational memory is so rare, I see so many people assume the past was the same as the present. They don't comprehend how we, in the past half century, created new kinds of poverty and desperation and degradation, how we broke things, and that there was a time before so many people and things were broken this way. Without that knowledge it is hard to imagine unbrokenness. Recognizing a constellation helped those escapees find freedom, even as they journeyed into the unknown. Like them, we must recognize patterns and choose directions.

This is a time when the baseline is slipping, when we risk forgetting what used to be and accept the chaos and devastation replacing it. This is a time when we will decide to move away from the catastrophe that the Age of Fossil Fuels has turned out to be, or not; will orient ourselves toward the landmarks of stability or become castaways adrift on a sea of escalating change.

The stories of climate change are Russian dolls, the words inside the thoughts inside the feeling inside the experience inside the local impact of this global warping and wrecking of the patterns on which we relied. They are testimony that this is not an abstract crisis; it is written on the hearts and sometimes on the graves of the people of the world in our time. It manifests in impacts in this village, that farm, that city, this home, that stream, this forest, that person who dies defending the forest, that person who flees the destruction of the forest and its defenders, that woman who gives birth too soon.

Usually, we want a story to be complete; we want to know how it ended. But we are writing in a moment when we do not know where we go from here, when we are trying to enlist popular will in overcoming the fossil fuel and status quo interests to turn us away from more devastation to more restoration of the patterns we are breaking down with such pain, with such tolls, in story after story here. We are writing stories that are not markers to say, "We got here," but compasses to say, "Press on in this direction."

In a black-and-white photograph, two figures draped in pale shawls so they faintly resemble clouds or icebergs or waterfalls themselves sit facing the sandy shore of an ocean. We see their shawls, their backs. If we imagine them sitting before the Anthropocene had fully announced itself, they sit and contemplate what seems like the great eternal churning of a sea whose inexhaustible stability we once believed in as devoutly as anything. Two women sit on the sandy shore of an ocean in our time, and they contemplate chaos, unpredictability, losses, an ocean changed in its inhabitants, its currents, its temperature, its pH, its shorelines, its storms. . .

May our efforts in the present make a time when two women sit by the sandy shore of an ocean and contemplate what we have done to reverse the damage of the late Age of Fossil Fuels, of how humanity put itself in harness to pull in the opposite direction, toward alignment with the plants that sequestered carbon and exhaled oxygen, toward making peace with nature after centuries of war, toward restoration, toward the stories of how it was that may stand as stories of how it could be. Toward the ways of those people who did so little harm in this era when some—especially in my own country—and the institutions they created did so much.

We were guided by stories, the old ones passed on, the new ones we made like rafts in a flood, the ones we told like water to pour on fire. Stories arose from this time, of those who did what was needed and those who stood in the way, and those who changed minds with their stories, of those new stories in which we saw a new heaven, a new Earth, and a new humanity. The stories of inseparability in which "we" meant forests and oceans and strangers on other islands as well as those around us, the stories that carried us through that time and into this one so unlike what came before.

The sky is full of forests.

On Letting Go of Certainty in a Story That Never Ends

The price of oil as I write (on Monday, April 20, 2020), or rather the benchmark of West Texas crude oil with May delivery, is negative $37 a barrel, and while there had been recent predictions that we were heading this way, it is still a wild event and not one most who weren't studying the context carefully could've foreseen. "Owing largely to a quirk in the way that oil prices are set, the May benchmark actually fell into negative territory, suggesting people who had oil to sell were willing to pay to have it taken off their hands," noted the *New York Times*. I had been watching, I'd heard predictions this was going to happen, because this was foreseeable a few weeks beforehand, but probably inconceivable a few months before when oil was at sixty dollars a barrel.

The unforeseen happens regularly; and then, not a few people forget that it does and look forward to a foreseeable future all over again and pretend they foresaw what surprised them, flatten the bump back into their smooth version of reality. We can make informed guesses, and the oil decline went down a well-marked path, but these brief yet significant negative numbers were still remarkable, foreseeable in the short term, but wild in the long.

When the pandemic began in earnest in this country, and the schools were closed in my region, I hoped to aid the parents of my nephews and great-nieces by coming over and doing stuff with the kids. Then, the new rules of the game meant that our households could not blend. I began reading fairytales online in part as a way to reach out to them and anyone else who wanted to listen, and also because fairytales felt like the right kind of narrative for the moment.

It turned out a lot of people wanted to hear fairytales for the four weeks I kept the series running, and it was nice for me too, with the various forms of contact—emoticons streaming across the live feed, chat and other responses from people I knew and people I didn't, the shoutout each time to a long list of kids and a few adults, from Manitoba to Louisiana, and the return to stories I loved, discovery of stories I didn't, and chance to reframe some that were troubling (I sent the protagonist of "The Little Mermaid" back to her sisters and took a detour from Theseus's version of the story of the Labyrinth to Jorge Luis Borges's minotaur-eye view and speculations on Ariadne's perspective).

Reading stories was a way of being with people even while most of us couldn't be with many people, and because even the most unfamiliar stories (I dug into Italo Calvino's big compendium of Italian folktales and Greg Sarris's Native Californian just-so stories) had the familiar rites of Once Upon a Time, when animals and even rivers and stones talked and genies came out of lamps and fishes granted wishes. The fairytale outcomes are more or less foregone, at least to the extent that the protagonist will make it out alive, but the route there and the nature of those protagonists is what seemed right for the moment.

Underneath all the trappings of talking animals and magical objects and fairy godmothers are tough stories about people who are marginal, neglected, impoverished, undervalued, and isolated, and their struggle to find their place and their people. Fairytales are distinct from hero tales at their most banal, the stories in which exceptionally powerful, usually male figures defend and enlarge their power (and in which the power is often the power to harm that we call violence), which is why I was so impelled to shift over from Theseus to Asterion and Ariadne.

Possessed of no such capacity for superior force, fairytale characters are given tasks that are often unfair verging on impossible, imposed by the more powerful—climb the glass mountain, sort the immense heap of mixed grain before morning, gather a feather from the tail of the firebird. They are often mastered by alliances with other overlooked and undervalued players—in particular, old women (who often turn out to be possessed of supernatural powers) and small animals, the ants who sort the grain, the bees who find the princess who ate the honey, the birds who sing out warnings. Those tasks and ordeals and quests mirror the difficulty of the task of becoming faced by the young in real life and explore the powers that most of us have: alliance, persistence, resistance, innovation. Or the power to be kind and the power to listen—to name two powers that pertain to storytelling and to the characters told of in these particular stories.

I often told my listeners that we were ourselves in the middle of a fairytale, and that at that moment our difficult task was to stay home. My project was a way to contextualize the time and to color it with the brightness of these stories. We were in the middle and the end was not in sight. We were waiting, which is among the least favorite things to do for most people, when it means noticing that you have taken up residence in not knowing. We were in terra incognita, which is where we always are anyway, but usually we have a milder case of it and can make our pronouncements and stumble along and hope that no one remembers that the winner is the person we said would never win or the catastrophe or victory is the one we said was impossible.

To live in the middle of a story is to live in suspense and uncertainty about what will happen. That journey through uncertainty to certainty is the engine that drives a lot of feature films, so much so that plot spoiler warnings are given when films are reviewed, or the review takes elaborate detours around revealing the outcome. For some of these entertainments, once the outcome is known they lose their magic.

Maybe fairytales are better because you know, more or less, that the heroine will survive, but how exactly she'll knit stinging nettles into shirts to transform her eleven brothers back into human form from the swans they were turned into is suspenseful, so, between the certainty and uncertainty, there is a pleasurably tingling lingering. The novels I have loved most I have been happy to wander through again and again, already aware that Elizabeth gets Darcy or Pip doesn't get Estella, and I'm content that the very first sentence tells us that Colonel Aureliano Buendia will face a firing squad (though whether the execution goes through or not is a later plot point). But there's a kind of throwaway potboiler where plot is an itch that seems irresistible to scratch, and the scratching of that itch is the main pleasure the book offers. Ocean Vuong remarked, at a talk at City Arts and Lectures in San Francisco, that plot is a woodchipper into which we throw characters.

Books have plots, because they are finite and authored; the world has an infinite number of authors, of whom you are one, and the surprising outcomes are often due to underestimated agents, such as the nonviolent protesters who toppled the Eastern Bloc regimes in 1989, or to the potential of new viruses that epidemiologists anticipated and most of the rest of us overlooked. Among the stories I read aloud was "Stone Soup," in which a trio of poor soldiers returning from a war convince the stingy villagers to contribute a little and a little more to a cauldron of boiling water, until a rich soup (and more vibrant community) that nourishes them all has been created.

But we pretend that life, like art, has plots and that we know how the story ends, whether it's an election or a cultural shift or the outcome of any major event, and we often err not on the side of caution but on the side of conventionality: the future will look like the present. This is why the financiers who determine our economic reality have been unable to fully comprehend the extraordinary decline of the fossil fuel industry, leaving them and their clients holding many worthless bags.* But the present only looks incomprehensible to those who ignore the past, which is full of the strange and unpredictable things that transpired to create the present, reminders of how often destiny hangs by a thread and turns on a dime, how often the unexpected happens anyway.

Martin Luther King Jr.'s "I Have a Dream" speech was not scripted; it came about because Mahalia Jackson called out to him as he was partway through a more pedestrian, scripted speech, "Tell them about the dream, Martin! Tell them about the dream!", and he pushed the paper aside and shifted into the more prophetic voice of that greatest of American speeches. It almost didn't happen—she was bold enough to call out in a historic moment; he could've

---

* Of course, when this piece was written, in 2020, the rebound in fossil-fuel prices prompted by the Putin regime's February 2022 invasion of Ukraine was likewise unforeseen, as was the way it hastened Europe's transition to renewable energy. So, for that matter, was the speed with which solar and wind energy would proliferate as prices plummeted beyond all forecasts, and technical problems such as battery storage and transmission were addressed with some success.

On Letting Go of Certainty in a Story That Never Ends

ignored her, but somehow he dared to listen and was nimble enough to improvise in front of that vast crowd in the nation's capital.

Perhaps the devastation of such a pandemic was too hard to believe, seemed too improbably unlike recent history, which is why governments that were warned of the possibility and then the inception did so little to prepare for it. When it comes to real life, this state of unknowing is both normal and so wildly uncomfortable that we engage in foolish and delusional imitations of knowing, whether it's trusting untrustworthy authorities or making pronouncements about outcomes with no particular basis in fact, knowledge, or history.

Years ago, when I began writing about a variety of hope that is inextricable from uncertainty—a sense that we don't know what will happen but we might have room to participate in determining what will happen—I ran into this false omniscience again and again, and found that a lot of people liked certainty, even grim certainty, more than the genuine uncertainty about what would happen next. If you pretend the future is preordained, you don't have to do anything. If you pretend you're in a small familiar room, you don't have to look up like Prince Andrei does, badly injured and lying on the battlefield in that scene in *War and Peace*, and wondering why he hadn't seen the sky before.

He recovers, and, in a later scene,

> He looked up at the sky to which Pierre had pointed, and for the first time since Austerlitz saw that high, everlasting sky he had seen while lying on that battlefield; and something that had long been slumbering, something that was best within him, suddenly awoke, joyful and youthful, in his soul. It vanished as soon as he returned to the customary conditions of his life, but he knew that this feel-

ing which he did not know how to develop existed within him. . . . Though outwardly he continued to live in the same old way, inwardly he began a new life.

That sense of vastness offers him, and I believe each of us, something, even though it's made of nothing you can hang on to.

In the fairytales I chose, the protagonists are not powerful in any conventional way, but they are active participants in their fate, leaving the familiar, taking risks, changing their lives, finding people worth connecting to, reaching out to help others, who will help them in turn. It turns out that the powers that matter are attentiveness, innovative thinking, and alliance building. They change their fate, which is to say it's not fate or destiny at all but an unwritten future that they seize authorship over. They don't know what will happen, but they launch into uncertainty with the energy of participants.

One of the things I returned to again and again in the storytelling is how you find spaciousness when confined to small spaces. In one session, I referenced my friend Jarvis Masters, who has, during decades in solitary confinement on death row in San Quentin, found ways to reach beyond his cell, to become a Buddhist practitioner connected to lamas and fellow practitioners in the world beyond, to form friendships, a writing life with publishers and readers who write back to him, lives he's touched and helped. He has created spaces to inhabit imaginatively, both within himself and beyond the prison.

Sometimes I could see, as I read the stories, that a thousand people were online with me, and I would propose that if we were all inside the same story and the story was being heard in a thousand rooms then we were somehow in a thousand-room palace together, and I would find a spaciousness in the tale and the connection to unseen others that felt a little like Prince Andrei's sky and hoped that others found it with me. Once, Jarvis called while I was gearing up to tell genesis stories by Subcomandante Marcos and Eduardo Galeano, and I put him on speakerphone and he joined us for a while, and those thousand people got to hear his vibrant, joyous laugh at what he considered, once again, my ridiculousness. We were all in that moment in the unexpected together, and it was a good place to be.

Familiarity is a life raft or some floating trash we might mistake for a life raft, but the task isn't to try to bellyflop onto the flotsam; it's to swim. We are in the ocean and time is fluid and the waves will keep coming and there is a distinct possibility that this is okay. A little like Li Po's poem about Chuang Tzu dreaming he's a butterfly dreaming he's Chuang Tzu, we are maybe dolphins dreaming that the clarity and dry solidity of the desert is our natural habitat rather than where we'd scorch and wither, are beings under Prince Andrei's illimitable sky sometimes yearning to be back in the box of the familiar and the predictable—though sometimes that's the house of love and the space we share with those we care about. Sometimes the right story is a bridge between the illimitable sky and the comfort of the intimate and an invitation to travel freely between them.

The part of the poem about the man who is the butterfly and the dream that is the life is often cited, but the rest is not. As one translation has it:

> Who can tell the end of the endless changes of things?
> The water that flows into the depth of the distant sea
> Returns anon to the shallows of a transparent stream.
> The man, raising melons outside the green gate of the city,
> Was once the Prince of the East Hill.

As I finish this, my friend Sam calls up and shows me on his phone his three-year-old son, my godson, jumping across a narrow stream that feeds a Texas river overhung with green trees, again and again, absorbed in his task of becoming, under a deep blue sky.

Tortoise at the Mayfly Party

These days I think of myself as a tortoise at the mayfly party. By that, I mean I try to see the long trajectory of events leading to the present moment, because it takes time to see change, and understanding change is essential to understanding politics and culture, let alone trying to participate in them. The short view generates incomprehension and ineffectuality.

Events, like living beings, have genealogies and evolutions, and to know those means knowing who they are, how they got there, and who and what they're connected to. If you follow them in either real time or the historical record, you can often see power that emerges from below and ideas that move from the margins to the center. You can see how it all works. Yet, these trajectories and genealogies are often left out of the news, the conversation, and, apparently, the conception of how something came to pass.

Change itself becomes invisible when your timeframe is shorter than that change, and the short-term view breeds defeatism and despair. Not long ago, people would announce to me that feminism had failed, apparently unable to recognize the extraordinary changes in the legal and cultural status of women over the past half century, or assuming that dismantling millennia of patriarchy was a simple task that should be all wrapped up in a few decades. We have just begun.

Forgetting is everywhere. Take the Biden administration's August 2023 announcement of a broad package of student loan relief. If you didn't follow the history, you could believe that it was a gift from above rather than an achievement long fought for from below. If you did follow it, you would have remembered how student debt emerged as a focus in 2011's Occupy Wall Street uprising. By raising up the voices of those crushed by debt and decrying the system that crushed them, it changed the national conversation.

Nevertheless, as soon as Occupy began, pundits were asserting it was a failure, and when the Zuccotti Park presence in Lower Manhattan was violently broken up by police in November 2011, they declared that it was over. But even when the rock's on the bottom of the pool, the ripples are still spreading.

Occupy's impact had just begun. It inspired other occupations far beyond New York City, some of them outside the United States. Across the country, police-accountability groups, solidarity organizing with foreclosure victims and the unhoused, and many other progressive projects emerged. Some of them lasted. One of them was the Debt Collective, founded in 2012. It has successfully taken on all forms of debt—housing, medical, and educational—and begun to organize to abolish debt directly, campaign for debt abolition and legal changes, and draw public attention to the devastating cruelty of the system. In 2015, the Debt Collective announced that a student debt strike it organized had initiated "an ongoing campaign that has helped win changes to federal law and over $2bn in student debt abolition to date." Activists made student debt a public issue, then it became part of the Biden campaign's platform, and that, ultimately, led to a series of debt-relief measures.

The year the Debt Collective started that campaign, the Supreme Court recognized marriage equality as a constitutional right.

The mayfly version would have seen that right as likewise handed down from above rather than built from below. But the court merely gave legal force to long-term campaigns that encouraged and built on broader shifts in acceptance and support of queer rights and inclusion. To see those shifts, you also have to remember what things were like beforehand.

Early in this country's history, John Adams wrote to Thomas Jefferson that the war of independence from the British throne was not the revolution: "The revolution was in the minds of the people and this was effected from 1760 to 1775 ... before a drop of blood was shed at Lexington." It's an assertion that the crucial change came through culture, through beliefs and values, that the most important territory to take is in the imagination. Once you create a new idea of what is possible and acceptable, the seeds are planted; once it becomes what the majority believes, you've created the conditions in which winning happens. It may be the least tangible—but most important—part of a campaign. Ideas are powerful and dangerous, as their enemies know, and everyone else often forgets.

One of the joys of being a tortoise is watching the slow journey of ideas from the margins to the center, seeing what is invisible, then deemed impossible, become widely accepted. The other day, the Salt Lake City *Tribune* editors called for draining Lake Powell, the now failing reservoir created sixty years ago by erecting Glen Canyon Dam, and for making its beautiful canyonlands into a new national park. That was considered an outrageous idea twenty years ago. The city of Oakland just announced plans to return five acres of open space to its original Ohlone owners, an act modest in scale but huge as a sign of how Native American land rights have gained recognition.

If people are shortsighted about the past, so they are about the future—a lot of complaining about the incompleteness of the student loan reform and cancellation was met with the Debt Collective's vow that they were far from done. That nearly all change is incremental and even a comprehensive victory usually has intermediary steps preceding it is one of the things that disappears in the short view. Imperfect and frustrating though those steps may be, they can still lead us to our destination. We can't reach the summit without climbing the mountain.

Perhaps some of this is built into the news cycle, which tends to report on events as sudden ruptures rather than the consequence of long-term forces. More of it may come from the attachment to the idea of revolution, of everything changing overnight, though it's no longer sensible, if it ever was, to believe regime change can change everything. The long revolutions around gender, nature, race, and the rest have, in our time, been incremental and largely cultural in means, even as they produce concrete ends.

Perhaps the problem is embedded in the very word *news*, as in *new*. In the sense that everything has a history, nothing is entirely new. (Even mayflies live for a year or two underwater as larvae before they emerge into the air for their few days of winged life.) I have been a witness to and sometimes a participant in change, and again and again I've seen people fail to recognize change, believe change is impossible, walk away prematurely, dismiss those who are trying, because of this lack of perspective.

The mayfly view is of a perpetual present in which the order of things is largely immutable or change is abrupt and incomprehensible. Those who are unable to see change are unable to strategize. Conservatives have been recognized for their long-term strategy, building power from the ground up, taking over local government, winning state races to take over state legislatures to control redistricting to gerrymander their way to minority power in the federal government, bending democracy into something worse.

Happily, they're not the only ones with tenacity. The examples are everywhere. In 2020, after thirty-one years of organizing, the coalition of ranchers, Native Nevadans, and other rural people who came together as Great Basin Water Network finally defeated Las Vegas's attempt to extract the water from one of the driest places on the continent. The plan would have taken 58 billion gallons of water annually from arid eastern Nevada, devastating wildlife and rural communities. As Eric Siegel's report in *High Country News* summarized it, "The Vegas Pipeline, had it succeeded, threatened to make a dust bowl of 305 springs, 112 miles of streams, 8,000 acres of wetlands, and 191,000 acres of shrubland habitat, almost all of it on public lands." Siegel quoted the Western Shoshone tribal elder Delaine Spilsbury, who declared, "Never give up the ship. Never. That's the kind of feeling that I think most of us had. Just do the best we can and let's make something happen, even if it does take forever."

It didn't take forever, but it took decades. For much of that time it would have been easy to look at the struggle and conclude that it was doomed or losing because it hadn't won. You could say the same of many other campaigns, including the student-led movement to get Harvard University to divest from fossil fuels, which took ten years to reach victory in 2021. As my friend Astra Taylor of the Debt Collective remarked to me when I congratulated her, "We're all losers until we win."

Another of my friends, Joe Lamb, is a poet and arborist who sports a T-shirt that says: "70 is young for a tree." In a recent essay about the epic tree-planting program that was part of the New Deal's effort to stop the erosion that had produced the Dust Bowl, he wrote, "We need to remember that we can learn from and repeat the successes of our past." It was a gorgeous revision of the old "Those who forget history are doomed to repeat it."

There are past victories you want to repeat, or build on, or learn from. Which is why understanding how they unfold is so essential, recognizing that an oak was once an acorn and then a spindly sapling, remembering this law was once a radical idea and then a campaign. That means seeing the world like a tortoise, not a mayfly.

In Praise of the Meander

This summer, a day after a promising thunderstorm, my friend Greg took me mushroom hunting in the New Mexico mountains, where he's been collecting them for forty years or more. If we'd tracked the routes we took, they would've resembled how toddlers scribble across a piece of paper, back and forth, back and forth, with a bit of round and round. We were looking at the ground, unhurried, trying to discern boletus mushrooms in the moist leaf litter, bending down to inspect and occasionally collect. I was detouring to admire the wildflowers in the little meadows punctuating the aspen and pine forest, and he was naming all the species of fungi and teaching me what to look for and vetting every mushroom that got plucked from the earth and popped in his sack.

Most of the time I go into such landscapes, I walk or run, cutting a line through the landscape, but I learned, in the years when I used to gather gallons of blackberries in the tree-shaded gulch through which a creek ran, that there's another kind of depth achieved by moving slow, seeing close-up, lingering, living in detail. You're not trying to get somewhere else but to know better where you are.

Some books have a single storyline, and they pass briskly through the landscape, often to a destination that doubles as payoff, such as "What the hell will Jane do with Rochester?" or "Who got the Eustace diamonds?" Or, they tread a wide, familiar road that is the chronology of a life—a movement, a war, or some other event. Other books—some of mine, I hope—are, instead, trying to map the surrounding territory and understand where we are. That is, such books are not linear, not built around a single chronology—in fact, they are often not structured around chronology at all. But, just as a mushroom hunter is neither lost nor without purpose, these books are not without structure or direction. Why not explore the terrain rather than cutting a swathe through it? Why not meander and see what lies alongside? Such books are concerned not so much with what happens but with what it means; they are less about destination than meaning revealed along the way.

Though I'm overall grateful for the reception of my book *Orwell's Roses*, reviewers have called it "a collection of essays" a number of times, which suggests a failure to recognize structure or internal cohesion if it is not tightly focused on a single figure or a chronological sequence. To me, that's like calling your family a collection of people or a tree a collection of sticks. "Collection" implies a bunch of disparate or unrelated things gathered up—collected, but not necessarily integrated or belonging together (and "essays" suggests that they're freestanding items rather than chapters). A book that is nonlinear may not be a string of pearls, but it might be the facets of a diamond or the bones in a skeleton, and Adam Hochschild delighted me by beginning a public conversation with me about the book by saying, "I think your book has the structure of a rosebush."

Of course, even a lot of old novels, let alone new ones, are not so linear. *Moby-Dick* is a book about a quest or chase, and hardly anything is more linear than that. But Melville is not in a rush, so his tome is interleaved with musings and chapters on nautical matters and, famously, "the whiteness of the whale." In pursuing one goal (or whale), Captain Ahab is in violation of the official purpose of the voyage of the *Pequod*, which is supposed to be a quest for many whales, not one. His singlemindedness is alarming until it's catastrophic; it's as though the book is a conflict between Melville's and Ishmael's broad interests and Ahab's narrow one, as though the recursive digressions and asides are, *Tristam Shandy*–style, trying to delay the devastation brought on by Ahab's vengeful obsession.

Time jumps, fragments, backward glances, and parallel subjects are familiar in novels, but somehow some readers seem to find them unrecognizable in a work of nonfiction that nevertheless constitutes a whole and is written in chapters that build on or inform each other. I'm not worried about my book, but I do want everyone to recognize that structures take many forms, and God knows there are plenty of nonfiction examples out there. Primo Levi's *The Periodic Table*, which narrates his life before and during his time in Auschwitz through chapters titled after the periodic elements he knew so well as a chemist, is not a collection of essays, and neither is Annie Dillard's *For the Time Being*, which brings together scraps of information about the same subjects again and again, like Bach's *Goldberg Variations*, to explore theological questions that are never quite asked outright. For that matter, *Walden* is organized by thematic chapters, because there's not much plot to Thoreau's spending some time in a shack on Emerson's woodlot. But they're definitely chapters, united by an interwoven exploration of place and meaning.

David Graeber and David Wengrow's magisterial history *The Dawn of Everything* is roughly chronological, but it is also a brilliant dismantling of the idea that human history has itself been a linear narrative—an inevitable march from innocence to corruption, from hunter-gatherers to agriculture to urbanism, from simplicity to complexity. It proposes that human beings are instead endlessly experimental. People tried on different economic and social arrangements, or mixed them up. Some peoples tried agriculture and went back to hunting and gathering. Similarly, not only was there no inevitable evolution from one form of social organization to another, but some cultures also went back and forth seasonally between forms, as they gathered and dispersed.

The funny thing is that *Orwell's Roses* loosely proceeds according to the chronology of Orwell's life and writing, though, as the title indicates (or at least as I intended it to indicate), it's a book about roses, too, as emblems, commodities, as members of the plant kingdom, and as things tended, enjoyed, and written about by Orwell. It begins again and again, seven times in seven sections, with variations on the opening sentence, "In the year 1936, a writer planted roses." What did it mean that this particular person planted and tended these particular flowers, right after his time amid the slums and coal mines in England's industrial north, not long before he went to Spain to fight fascism in the Spanish Civil War?

I wanted to answer the question posed by that act of planting roses, or rather to explore it, since you can broaden rather than narrow in the pursuit of meaning, and an answer is often a capstone or a terminus, part of the fiction that there is one answer rather than many. The structure of *Orwell's Roses* is akin to taking seven walks from the same starting point. To explore that question meant going out into Orwell's world and our own to situate the one act in its many contexts and possibilities. I learned from labyrinths that to get to the center you turn away from it again and again as you follow the windings that will, in the end, take you to the center. In Hokusai's *Thirty-Six Views of Mount Fuji*, most of the woodblock prints show the famous conical peak, but one shows pilgrims climbing a Fuji that is the very ground under their feet. You can't see the mountain's form while you're on the mountain. There are subjects you can better understand through analogy, context, parallels, the view from the distance, rather than via direct and dogged pursuit.

There was a very fun moment in the television serial *Ted Lasso*'s second season, in which junior coach Nate Shelley is worried someone else will take credit for his idea, and the laconically erudite Coach Beard replies, "You know, we used to believe that trees competed with each other for light. Suzanne Simard's fieldwork challenged that perception, and we now realize that the forest is a socialist community. Trees work in harmony to share the sunlight." He is more or less observing that we are shifting from the hyperindividualism of coldwar capitalism, social Darwinism, and a host of other sadly Hobbesian views to a recognition that the world is made of interconnected and interdependent systems rather than isolated objects.

In a lot of fields, from psychology to economics to ecology, people are noticing that cooperative and collective rather than competitive relationships seem to be how we're wired and what works. Simard's own work is on the way forests share underground through mycorrhizal fungal networks, which knit the trees and fungi together into an interspecies whole. Her wonderful book *Finding the Mother Tree* braids the story of her personal and professional life with her scientific work and its implications. The postmodern philosophers Deleuze and Guattari proposed, in a passage a little unfair to trees, "Any point of a rhizome can be connected to anything other, and must be. This is very different from the tree or root, which plots a point, fixes an order."

Rhizomatic became an important word for nonlinear literary structures, but, as with so much philosophy, they seem to be thinking about it in opposition an imaginary or abstracted tree. Though there are regularly branching family trees and other uses of the information-tree structure, trees themselves can take many forms, and some boughs dip down to touch the earth and sink new roots into it, sometimes many trunks grow from one rootstock, and where I live trees dripping in the lichen we call Spanish moss, trees covered in mosses, serving as habitats for other species, trees sculpted by the wind, entangled with each other and with vines are all familiar. An oak has one trunk but many radiating branches and subbranches, often zigzagging like lightning, all the way to leafy twigs spreading in all directions, and I have often loved how they reach out to make a hemisphere of sorts. Simard's work tells us that even the trees that above ground looked like linear independent structures were often, underground, part of great dense cooperative tangles that also included fungi and microbes and invertebrate animals.

The literary equivalent is maybe not a tangle but a recognition that everything exists in context, that your subject may be the system rather than the individual, the network of ideas and meanings that reach out like mycorrhizal fungi to connect things and circulate their nutrients. Those mushrooms Greg and I were picking were just the fruiting bodies of great underground networks, and you probably didn't think I could come full circle here, but I just did. I was meandering but not lost.

Insurrectionary Aunthood

"Auntie is also an ethic, a way of being with others…"
—Kareem Khubchandani

If aunthood at its best is a form of mutual aid, perhaps mutual aid at its best is a form of aunthood, and both can be forms of resistance to patriarchy and capitalism. That is, they can be more fluid, less linear, less transactional ways in which love, resources, and power move in and out and through a life, a group, a family, a society. They can embrace the idea of the systems of interconnection in defiance of the ideology of isolation. In that nonlinear spirit, I want to take a roundabout route to the question of what exactly is mutual about mutual aid, and what its opposites and opponents are, and why aunts matter. If they are also marginal then that's a sign that the margins and who's in them are what matter, and perhaps that they're the same as the liminal.

This essay was written as part of an anthology about the Auntie Sewing Squad, the mask-sewing mutual aid group Los Angeles performance artist Kristina Wong founded in March 2020, which grew into a community that, as of 2024, still stays in touch. As of mid-2021, the group, which grew to about eight hundred members, had sewn about three hundred thousand cloth masks for distribution to the most vulnerable and devalued in the pandemic.

I. NUCLEAR MONUMENTS

One evening in July of 2020, I went walking near Truckee, California, and to my surprise found that across the stream that ran through the meadow stood a monument to the Donner Party. Atop the tall plinth, a huge bronze man holds one hand to his brow, as if scouting the horizon, and the usual pioneer wife-mother stands next to him, as these figures usually do, with the usual babe at her breast. In this iteration, a crouching girl-child clings to the man's leg, and the implication is that he is independent and the other three are dependents. "Virile to risk" begins the plaque on the plinth, whatever that means about the blundering party that, thanks to mistakes and discord and poor judgment, got itself stranded in this location over the long snowy winter of 1846–47 and is most famous because of the cannibalism to which some of the stranded members resorted.

It reminded me of another pioneer monument I'd seen four years earlier, when I'd gone to report on the resistance to the Dakota Access Pipeline led by the Standing Rock Sioux. I followed a Native youth–led protest to the statehouse in Bismarck, North Dakota, and, on the vast lawn in front of the building, there was a similar pioneer monument the protesters were obliged to confront. Another resolute bronze man towered over another woman with babe in arms on one side of him; on the other, instead of a clinging girl, was a young man with a hand on a wagon wheel. But it was at the Donner memorial that I realized these were—as well as monuments to white invaders of Native lands—affirmations of the nuclear family.

The standard-issue nuclear family is, of course, a heterosexual couple and their unfledged offspring, ruled over by the father/husband; it is, in other words, a breeding pair, a labor arrangement, and a power structure. It is how family has long been celebrated in the US, in ways that erase or diminish or disparage the extended family and alternative family structures and the need for membership in larger social configurations. Though the Donner Party included single men and some extended and blended families, the nuclear family was the portable minimum unit for production and reproduction, and westward migration often shriveled social units down to this minimalist formulation. Both Laura Ingalls Wilder, in her *Little House on the Prairie* series, and Hamlin Garland, in his *Son of the Middle Border*, recount how their fathers tore their wives and children away from the security and conviviality of extended family into lonely incursions across the West.

Garland wrote, when his father uprooted his family for the fifth time, "My mother, thus widely separated from her kin, resigned herself once more to the thought of founding a new home. The border line had moved on, and my indomitable Dad was moving with it. I shivered with dread of the irrevocable decision thus forced upon me." The isolation of the nuclear family fortified the absolute authority of the patriarch; they were an amplification of his individualism or an accessory to it. Perhaps these monuments were erected across the American West in the twentieth century because the rise of wage labor and uprooting in search of work had made the stripped-down family the norm: nineteenth-century figures used to reaffirm twentieth-century social structures.

The nuclear family as portrayed in these statue groupings is a closed and self-sufficient unit, with one power center, like the nucleus of the atom from which the term is drawn. The extended family, by contrast, might have multiple and dissenting power centers, as might a family woven into the larger community, or one in which women as well as men were decision-makers (or both heads of household were the same gender). All of these alternative forms, to say nothing of queer chosen family and contemporary alternative models, are more fluid, more multicentered, more negotiable.

The nuclear family is rendered monstrous in another way when it is imagined and portrayed as where love, compassion, care, responsibility begin and end, and imagines all meaningful relationships as based on the fixed obligations of parents, particularly mothers, to children, children to parents, spouses to each other (but especially wives to husbands). Conservative ideology's emphasis on the strong family can be inverted to see that it is also an emphasis on weak ties and commitments elsewhere. It's a kind of contract law and a kind of emotional capitalism, of return on investment and ownership: transactional love.

II. IN PRAISE OF AUNTHOOD

Enter aunts. An aunt is by title and definition tangential, liminal, and maybe a tad marginal or at least peripheral: not a parent or spouse but the sibling of a parent, often imagined as older, of the age when women tend to become partially invisible (though I became an aunt three weeks after I turned eighteen). If the nuclear family is a sealed container, she is, ideally, a window, a door, a key baked into a cake, a messenger coming and going, oscillating between presence and absence, insider and outsider.

Colm Tóibín writes of nineteenth-century aunts in English novels, "One of the other purposes of aunts is that they allow for dramatic entrances and departures. All through the nineteenth century, aunts breach the peace and lighten the load." There are aunts in residence, yet the aunt is often, instead, someone who can be counted upon to show up, who also departs—and, with arriving and departing, she literally opens doors and brings in what was absent, and sometimes provides a place other than the pressure cooker of the family home.

In Toni Morrison's novel *Song of Solomon*, the protagonist, Milkman, has an icily ambitious father who has isolated his wife and children—and, across town, a bootlegger aunt whose all-female household, with its erotic energy, its traffic of customers, its violation of rules and indifference to rank, is the antithesis of the father's house. At the end, Milkman realizes, of his aunt, "Now he knew why he loved her so. Without ever leaving the ground, she could fly." But what's significant here is maybe not just that Milkman's aunt is kinder and freer than his father but that she's influential, that impact is not linear, that the forces that shape us are often those that not only lie beyond the nuclear family but also contradict or offer escape from it.

An aunt can singlehandedly supply some of the virtues of the extended family as a source of kindness and care without having entered into the multiple obligations of the family for whom she cares, or the assigned benefits. Or, necessarily, the ideology and the official narrative. She is subversively without contract. Of course, aunts are sometimes outlaws and sometimes enforcers of laws. In Margaret Atwood's *The Handmaid's Tale*, aunt, as in Aunt Lydia, is an official category of female upholders of patriarchy, which raises the question of whether there is also a sort of auntarchy that aunts can uphold (and, certainly, the term antifascist gave rise to the shorthand antifa, which in turn gave rise to the pleasant offshoot term *auntiefa* or *Auntie Fa*).

Scholar and drag performer Kareem Khubchandani theorizes what he calls "auntology," the culture and power of aunties. He describes growing up, witnessing the aunties around his mother "doing feminist work without ever calling themselves feminists, just by supporting each other. This idea of the aunty—as someone who is the repository of culture and who tells us whether we're doing it right or wrong, who praises and affirms us—also has the potential to open up space for queerness."

Part of the logic of the nuclear family is that it exists to perpetuate the paternal line, the family name, the lineage—and it is linear. An aunt is outside this linearity. She might be from the same tree if she's a blood relation, but she's a different branch, and the aunties who are not blood relations are about other forms of affiliation and solidarity that don't show up on these maps. You could call them nonlinear. Linear is a straight line; outside the straight is the queer.

III. QUEER UNCLES (AND LICHENS)

Though outsiders pretend science is made purely of facts, it is always also a social mirror. Thus it was that Darwin's *The Origin of Species*, prompted by a voyage the decade before the Donner Party's blighted 1846–47 expedition and published the decade after, was used to reinforce linear and individualistic stories. Darwin's ideas were distorted into the social Darwinism that frames survival of the fittest as ferocious competition, argues that competition is natural and inevitable, and claims the most ruthless competitor wins (though for Darwin himself "fittest" meant best adapted to its environment, which is often about cooperative belonging rather than competitive domination). But social Darwinism took hold and was used to reinforce gender, class, and racial hierarchies and free-market ideologies. At the same time, the communal family labor of farming was being replaced by the wage labor that turned wives and children into economic dependents and helped standardize the nuclear family.

But there were other versions available. Only a decade after Darwin's *Origin of Species*, a Swiss botanist proposed the radical idea that lichens were not a single organism but a collaboration between two distinct entities, a fungus and an algae. He saw them as locked into a relationship that was parasitic and coercive. Not long after that, biologist Albert Frank coined the word *symbiosis* and argued that separate species—even separate kingdoms, fungi and plants—had mutually beneficial rather than exploitative relationships. Fungus scholar Merlin Sheldrake, in his book *Entangled Life*, notes that, like the lichen theory, this theory was fiercely attacked.

Another major dissent from social Darwinism came from Peter Kropotkin, who, though best known as a revolutionary and anarchist theorist, was also a distinguished naturalist and geographer. Kropotkin's *Mutual Aid: A Factor of Evolution* (published serially in the 1890s) argued that cooperation and collaboration were equally powerful forces in ensuring the survival of species and individual members of species. He had observed firsthand in the Asian far north that resources were not scarce and survival was not based on competition for them but on collective action to survive the harsh environment. His writing is also where the term *mutual aid*, in its social sense, comes from; he let stand the idea that culture reiterates nature while providing a radically different account of nature.

Since the sixties, new theories and studies have veered away from competition as a driving force to recognize the centrality of symbiosis and cooperation. In 1967, Lynn Margulis proposed that multicellular life itself was the result of two different kinds of single-celled organisms joining together billions of years ago. It was revolutionary as a narrative of convergence rather than divergence, collaboration rather than competition. She described what had previously been seen as distinct individuals in plant, animal, and fungus kingdoms as "metabolically complex communities of a multitude of tightly organized beings." The plurality meant that the borders between as well as within were blurrier, more trafficked, than they had been imagined to be in the ideology of individualism. Her ideas, widely rejected at the time, have largely prevailed.

By 2012, a trio of biologists could publish an essay titled "A Symbiotic View of Life: We Have Never Been Individuals." They noted that, like plant scientists before them, zoologists "are also finding that animals are composites of many species living, developing, and evolving together. The discovery of symbiosis throughout the animal kingdom is fundamentally transforming the classical conception of an insular individuality into one in which interactive relationships among species blurs the boundaries of the organism and obscures the notion of essential identity." They conclude, "We are all lichens."

Biologist David Griffiths picked up where they left off, arguing that lichens, organisms that are a kind of ongoing mutual aid, "potentially offer a queer way out of heteronormative narratives of human and non-human sexuality and sociality by decentering heterosexual biological reproduction as the *only* way that life (re) produces." He notes that myriad organisms are generative in various ways other than heterosexual reproduction: "Sexual reproduction and vertical inheritance are only part of the picture, and … it is a heteronormative misinterpretation of 'life' and 'nature' to overemphasize these." That is, there are other forces and ways of relating and sustaining and propagating life and shaping systems. The pioneer statues fall off their pedestals, the straight line of lineage curls and forks, the individual turns out to have been a gathering all along, the family tree becomes a forest. As for that forest—as ecologist Suzanne Simard's research demonstrates, the trees and fungi in it are collaborating in underground networks through which resources travel.

IV. ISOLATIONISTS AND INTERCONNECTIONISTS

These changes in the way biology is imagined and represented parallel changes in other areas of thought—including economics, psychology, neurology, sociology—that together constitute a more systemic, more interconnected worldview that emphasizes human empathy, sharing, and collaboration. Its antithesis is what I think of as "the ideology of isolation": fundamental to modern right-wing worldviews is the idea that nothing is connected to anything else, that actions either have no consequences or actors have no responsibility for consequences, the libertarian logic used for tax cuts, gun deregulation, the refusal to address climate change, and, in 2020, the furious refusal to comply with the actions that would limit the spread of Covid-19.

Isolationists and *interconnectionists* might be more useful terms for the political divides of our time than *left* and *right*. The isolationists deny the scientific and moral case for interconnection as fact and treat its mention as an affront, whether it's how human-produced carbon dioxide accumulating in the upper atmosphere changes the climate or how viruses circulate or how much oppression is the result of systemic rather than individual failure. You could describe the position as: "Nothing is mutual, there is therefore no justification for aid." The Covid-19 pandemic was, like the climate crisis, a reminder that we are interconnected and that what we do as individuals and together affects the whole; that's a scientific fact rather than a political position, but those who reject the facts treat them as political opinions (and in some versions of the libertarian worldview, everyone gets to have their own facts).

In that conflict, the Auntie Sewing Squad (ASS) was at the other end of the spectrum from the isolationists. ASS was not only supporting the value of masks in March, 2020, when medical experts were still waffling about their utility (in part because they took the Western/individualist position that masks were to protect the wearer rather than others), but also working to provide, eventually, tens of thousands of them for vulnerable strangers across the country. It was, as mutual aid in disaster often is, an endeavor to make up for institutional failures. What was maybe distinct about it was the form it took—hundreds of people, mostly women, majority women of color, particularly Asian American, separately cutting and sewing cloth masks at home, which would be gathered for distribution to marginalized, overlooked, and vulnerable populations, staying in touch through a Facebook group that became a vibrant place for practical tips, political discourse, humor, the forging of friendships, the organization of aid, and the display of extraordinarily beautiful arrays of masks (often batches of them in complementary colors and prints, spread out in fans, wreaths, and other patterns).

ASS constituted an exemplary project in forming new connections and community even during quarantine; in emphasizing self-care for the makers and supplying it as affection, praise, support, and gifts of food and handmade items, while those makers toiled on behalf of others—usually strangers they would never meet; in harnessing a traditionally feminine craft form made in private to radical social intervention in groups and public; in embracing political discourse as part of the project while other mask-making groups often avoided it; in transforming rage at institutional failure into kindness to those impacted by that failure; in continually reaching out to those in need with consciousness of the race, class, and gender politics in play; in making the specific project into a vessel for larger ideals; and in incorporating aesthetics—an appreciation for beautiful fabrics, colors, and craft—into a political project addressing public health.

At the other end of the spectrum was the insistence that wearing masks was an intolerable imposition and violation of rights, prompting a series of violent crimes, including murders, carried out by white men in response to being asked or told to wear masks, as well as mass protests by those (largely white conservatives) who saw masks as impinging on a form of personal freedom that was defined as being without obligation to others under any circumstances.

Writing about pandemic mutual aid in Taiwan, Chia-Hsu Jessica Chang declared, "In the modern/colonial world, we are disciplined to be lonely. The oppressors call this loneliness 'individuality.' They make us to believe that the body of an ideal individual is impermeable and intact. Therefore, we imagine the impermeable and intact spaces to safely contain our bodies, and we reify such spaces by cutting through places with racial, gender, and national borders.... We know that bordered spaces and individualized bodies are violent designs. We undo borders and create shared spaces. We do not only acknowledge, but also actively embrace our bodies' vulnerability and permeability."

A disaster, natural or otherwise—a flood, earthquake, war, pandemic—upsets the status quo and the usual order. The disaster is itself terrible, but it often opens up the possibility of change, because the authorities have failed and lost standing, because the need to solve problems is urgent and in the hands of unofficial people. Often, in providing that aid, people discover new capacities within themselves, and new alliances among themselves, so what is produced is not only aid but other senses of self, society, and possibility. This is the paradise built in hell, the other possibilities that come through the cracks in everyday life. The paradise lies in the fluid possibilities of emergent alliances, associations, and organizations, and the ways they network through the impacted area to circulate what's needed. And in both the deep kindness motivating that action and the agency and alliance that emerge.

What fails in a disaster is institutional authority—particularly when it has not sufficiently organized in advance to meet the demands, is corrupt and callous, or incompetent—but a disaster often overwhelms official capacity even from good government (for example, the San Francisco Fire Department, in the 1989 Loma

Prieta earthquake—impromptu volunteers were a crucial part of the response to the major fire that broke out). If official authority resembles the husband-father in a nuclear family, then it's the extended family and the neighbors who reach out to help and comfort and rebuild. This is why aunthood—with aunts and aunties as the closest outsiders—seems so resonant a framework for mutual aid.

V. MUTUALITIES

Shortly after Hurricane Katrina hit the Gulf Coast, New Orleans was hit by a largely unnatural catastrophe that was due both to infrastructure that failed as it was predicted to fail and a lack of evacuation plans beyond the every-man-for-himself order to go. Left behind was a largely poor, largely Black population that was also disproportionately young (mothers with small children) and old, the people without the resources to get themselves out of there. In this chaos, a couple of white Texans joined New Orleans residents Malik Rahim and Sharon Johnson when they asked for help with the white vigilantes threatening them and other Black people. The Texans had worked with Rahim on the case of the Angola Three, Black Panthers who had spent decades in solitary confinement, and Rahim was also a former Panther.

They formed a group they named Common Ground and chose as their slogan "Solidarity not charity," a phrase inspired by the Uruguayan writer Eduardo Galeano's statement "I don't believe in charity. I believe in solidarity. Charity is so vertical. It goes from the top to the bottom. Solidarity is horizontal. It respects the other person. I have a lot to learn from other people." This time around, I began to wonder about what makes disaster-time mutual aid mutual, since, in actuality, it's most often a one-way flow of goods and services. Perhaps it's not the specifics of the transaction but the belief that we are, as Martin Luther King Jr. once put it, "an inescapable network of mutuality, tied in a single garment of destiny." The Auntie Sewing Squad cut that garment into masks for those who needed it most, with the knowledge that the threads that sewed a mask also tied us all together beyond that one gift and garment.

To put it more directly, what is mutual in mutual aid is not in the goods and services delivered; it's in the underlying belief in the deep connections between those who give and those who receive. It is a deep belief in and commitment to inseparability: that my well-being is inseparable from yours and that, in caring for yours, I care for myself and, more than that, for the larger whole that is us, because we are in this together. That is, we are not mutual because of the exchange of aid; we aid each other because we are already mutual. The word *mutual* is often used in this context to mean symmetrical, as in a symmetrical exchange, a relationship of reciprocity, but mutual aid in the sense that ASS and Common Ground practice it isn't exactly this kind of mutual. It is more like the other meaning of the word—what we have in common before and beyond exchange: mutual friends, mutual feelings, a mutual fate.

Galeano also speaks of horizontality, a sense of equality between giver and recipient—in Spanish, *horizontalidad* became a crucial word in Argentina's 2001 financial disaster and insurrection as a way to describe relationships of mutuality and equality among the people taking care of each other and organizing neighborhoods and movements. Mutual aid is how lichens work, and how disaster relief works, and how societies that function work; it is the circulatory system, commons, and collaborations; it's how an aunt's gesture that might be seen as altruistic—going one way—is in a larger sense mutual. So, mutual aid can be described as specific acts, but those acts are in service of the maintenance or restoration of the whole.

Often, the failure of this interconnectedness, this mutuality, produces the disaster—in the case of the 2020 pandemic, the failure of a federal disaster response, including the supplying of masks and other protective equipment, the failure of a commitment to take care of the most vulnerable, greatly expanded the reach and impact of the pandemic. Mutual aid is also unofficial—as the government or large institutions fail, improvisational and emergent organizations, usually based in the impacted places or populations, succeed. This is often because of a responsiveness and an attunement that are in part about decentralized and grassroots—or horizontal—decision-making and community connections, as distinct from top-down models, in which those at the top lack the capacity, conceptually and practically, to respond to the intricacies of myriad changing situations.

This means recognizing the indirect, long-term, and incalculable benefits of actions. One source of my thinking is anthropologist David Graeber's writing on debt, in which he notes that the old idea was that traditional societies bartered, awkwardly, until money smoothed the transactions. He makes the case that, instead, goods and services circulated in complex ways that knit people together as a community; the transactions were never finished in the way that a cash transaction is, and neither were the relationships. Money is, in his telling, specifically a way to terminate a connection, while the other models of circulation strengthened and perpetuated the connections. That can include mutual aid.

So many histories are written like family histories, with a model of direct lineage—influences are whittled down to a linear narrative of a homogenous ancestry, ethnicity, nationality: creative people are influenced only by people in their own fields, public figures by public life, politics by the political, culture by the cultural. Impact is described as direct, immediate, or linear, or dismissed. It's a genealogical impulse that denies indirect effect, long-term consequence, and many forms of what could be called cross-pollination. New Orleans's Common Ground brought a radical critique to relief and its failures, to the racial politics of reconstruction, and to racism in the South in general, and the hundreds of young volunteers who came got educated and, as with projects such as Freedom Summer in Mississippi in 1964, took that education onward with them (as did youth who volunteered at a number of other progressive projects in the wake of Katrina).

Similarly, the resistance to the Dakota Access Pipeline catalyzed in the summer of 2016 by members of the Standing Rock Sioux tribe in South Dakota came out of Native commitment to protection of the land and water and the particular threat to the Standing Rock land and the Missouri River that runs through it. It became the biggest Native American gathering and dovetailed with the climate movement's commitment to stopping fossil-fuel pipelines and the recognition that climate justice is also racial justice. The fate of the pipeline advanced and was checked by legal decisions again and again, and the Standing Rock Lakotas' litigation continues. But if stopping the pipeline was the lineal and direct goal, the indirect consequences were far broader—and remarkable.

There were too many to count, but one was the apology, by ex-soldiers on their knees representing the four thousand veterans who had come in support, for what the US military had done to Native Americans over the centuries. Another was the inspiration to a young Latina New Yorker who had driven out with friends to join the encampments that fall of 2016; she decided, because of what she had seen and felt, to run for office, and when she won her primary in the summer of 2018, the nation and the world got acquainted with Alexandria Ocasio-Cortez, who has become a powerful voice for climate, racial, and gender justice. Native youth at Standing Rock, I was told in 2020 by a Standing Rock Lakota medic working with ASS auntie Constance Parng, had reaped hope and encouragement from what happened there. Nonnative people had gotten another round of antiracist education from the high-profile actions and the discussions about tribal sovereignty, violated treaties, and Lakota history.

Parng formed a long-term alliance with Standing Rock. After ASS expanded its role to provide large-scale shipments of supplies and sewing machines to the Navajo Nation, she brought news to the group of Standing Rock's need for medical supplies and equipment. That spun off into a project to equip medical teams on the reservation, and she worked with a Bay Area doctor and a medical nonprofit to fill those needs and support long-term medical capacity expansion. A three-ton shipment of medical supplies went to Standing Rock in October of 2020, two donated ambulances followed, and an ASS-led drive to provide winter clothing sent more than two thousand coats to Standing Rock and Pine Ridge between 2021 and 2023. As I joked to ASS founder Kristina Wong, in the end she may turn out to have made ambulances in South Dakota with a funky sewing machine in Los Angeles.

Organizations spring up suddenly—but, to use a fungal metaphor, just as mushrooms are only the visible, fruiting bodies of the larger fungus that was long there, underground, so emergent disaster mutual aid often arises out of networks that have long existed. In ordinary times, those organizations may exist for other reasons—as church groups or friendship networks; in extraordinary times, it turns out that the pleasure and leisure produced a safety net that can catch us when things fall apart. In those times of crisis, these networks often expand suddenly in ways that matter afterward. Other times, an emergent organization is like spores on the wind that may land in new places, sowing new life.

It is too soon to say what the Auntie Sewing Squad created, beyond tens of thousands of masks to help prevent the spread of this terrible new disease; friendships; a sense of purpose and capacity for resistance against the horror of the pandemic, its isolation, and the Trump administration's vicious failures; and a remarkable example of radical mutual aid. But you could say that the Auntie Sewing Squad took hold of the single garment of destiny of which Dr. King spoke and sewed it into protective masks, and that not only were miles of thread used to sew but other, less visible threads stitched together relationships of solidarity across the continent.

II.
Revisions

Despair Is a Luxury

When you take on hope, you take on its opposites and opponents—despair, defeatism, cynicism, and pessimism. And, I would argue, optimism. What all these enemies of hope have in common is confidence about what is going to happen, a false certainty that excuses inaction. Whether you feel assured that everything is going to hell or will all turn out fine, you are not impelled to act. All these postures undermine participation in political life in ordinary times and in the climate movement in this extraordinary time. They are generally both wrong in their analysis and damaging in their consequences.

Not acting is a luxury those in immediate danger do not have, and despair when it leads to inaction, something they cannot afford. But despair is all around us, telling us the problems are insoluble, we are not strong enough, our efforts are in vain, no one really cares, and human nature is fundamentally corrupt. Some push their view like evangelists not merely surrendering to defeat but campaigning vigorously on its behalf. I've encountered a lot of them since I began to talk and write about hope almost twenty years ago.

In 2003, I wrote an essay called "Hope in the Dark" that became the 2004 book of that title that I revised and updated in 2016. I was responding to the immediate crisis of the moment—the Bush administration's invasion of Iraq, which, like Putin's invasion of

Ukraine in 2022, is all about the ways that fossil fuel fuels despotism, violence, and corruption. What I saw all around me, in friends and allies and the US antiwar movement, was a series of leaps. They began with "We did not stop the war," which was true, though opposition delayed it and changed its shape, and went from there to a cascade of conclusions that were not true: "We didn't do anything; we have no power; we never win; we can't win."

What motivated me to write it wasn't only the desire to assuage the grief and sense of powerlessness and futility that arose when the war broke out. It was exhilaration from the sense of history and the theory of change I'd gathered as a witness and sometimes participant in history-making in the present, and as a student of the past. If you do not take the long view, take in time in large increments, you cannot see how campaigns build, how beliefs change, how what was once thought to be impossible or outlandish comes to be the status quo, and how the last half century has been an extraordinary period of change for society, beliefs, and values. Today may seem the same as yesterday, but this decade is profoundly different than the last, so you must take your measurements in large increments.

I had, in the dozen years before 2003, seen indigenous peoples of the Americas rise up, seize power, rewrite history, reclaim rights, language, pride, ceremony. I had an inkling that these peoples consigned to the past—told that they were doomed or already extinct and their ways were archaic—would be crucial leaders in the future we needed. That has come to pass in important ways, both conceptually and practically. Indigenous ideas about our inseparability from and responsibility to the natural world have reshaped the moral imaginations of many of the rest of us. Indigenous people are climate leaders and land protectors around the world.

These were descendants of people who faced, as my friend Yotam Marom recently wrote, the end of their world, and in important ways did not give up. As Julian Aguon, a climate activist and lawyer indigenous to Guam, recently put it, indigenous peoples are those who "have a unique capacity to resist despair through connection to collective memory and who just might be our best hope to build a new world rooted in reciprocity and mutual respect—for the earth and for each other. The world we need. The world of our dreams."

His emphasis on collective memory tells us what the theologian Walter Brueggeman put in another way: "Memory produces hope in the same way that amnesia produces despair." The past equips us to face the future; continuity of memory tells us we are both descendants and ancestors. Perhaps the astonishing changes of the past equip us to imagine that more lie ahead, and not to confuse the inability to imagine a future with the impossibility of having one.

There had been other events that had started to feed my sense of hope, including the unforeseen transformation of the Soviet satellite states of Eastern Europe in 1989, through nonviolent direct action after long years of organizing and then the disintegration of the Soviet Union in 1991, ending the Cold War itself. No one really saw it coming, which taught me that history is full of ruptures and surprises. Beyond that, I saw huge shifts in the status of women, people of color, people with disabilities, and queer people in my lifetime, thanks to movements acting on new ideas and values and to innumerable everyday acts of courage and revolt by individual members of those groups.

I saw how new ideas often travel from the margins and the shadows and move to the center, to the limelight, where people—judges, presidents, prime ministers, international bodies—make decisions. If you don't follow the sequence of events over years or decades, you can believe that these are the powerful handing down change rather than change that began outside and below and grew until the powerful were obliged to endorse it.

I saw that those who are supposed to be powerless—writers and scholars, grassroots organizers and movements, visionaries, the disparaged and overlooked—have changed the world again and again. I learned some of this firsthand as an antinuclear activist and a member, from 1992 to about 1995, of the Western Shoshone Defense Project, a land-rights campaign led by the matriarchal ranchers Mary and Carry Dann from their ancestral land in eastern Nevada.

And so, in the Bush era, I went on the road to try to, as Jesse Jackson had urged in his 1988 presidential campaign, "keep hope alive." I met with many kinds of responses—relief, joy, good questions, powerful stories, and sometimes also rage. The rage, to my surprise, seemed to come largely from middle-class white people. They seemed to see despair as a form of solidarity and hope as a betrayal. Underneath this was, so far as I could tell, the assumption that whatever cause was in question was doomed, so we could start mourning right away.

But you shouldn't mourn those who aren't dead. Doing so stuffs the living into coffins, at the very least in your imagination. Native North Americans, from the nineteenth century into the 1990s, were regularly told through artworks and by bureaucrats and signage in museums and national parks and history books that their cultural or literal demise was inevitable, that they were doomed or already gone. Nonnative people widely believed it. I have met Native people who were told to their faces that they and their culture were extinct. Those who said these things often saw themselves as sympathizing with those they regarded as history's victims, but they told this story in ways that reinforced it.

The same harmful story is told of frontline climate communities when they are told they cannot win and have no future, but as Aguon points out, they are themselves fiercely hopeful. Prophesies are always partly self-fulfilling; by promoting whatever outcome they describe, they make it more likely. In this, we can distinguish them from warnings, which assume the outcome is as yet undecided and urge us away from the worst version. *You could be annihilated* is a very different statement from *you will be annihilated*. One includes room to act, the other adds nails to the coffin.

For those of us whose lives are already easy, giving up means making those lives even easier, at least in terms of effort. For the directly impacted, giving up means surrendering to devastation. Giving up on their behalf is not solidarity. And I doubt that anyone in desperate straits has ever taken comfort in the idea that somewhere far safer, people are bitter and despondent on their behalf or have decided they are doomed.

The desperate are sometimes themselves embittered and exhausted but often stubbornly hopeful. Even if they would say they don't hope, their perseverance is itself a kind of hope, a refusal to surrender. Despair can be true as an emotion but false as an analysis. Even when it is realistic as an analysis, many still stand up and resist on principle. I've seen that spirit of defiance in frontlines climate communities in the present. It's why the Pacific Climate Warriors, who come from fifteen South Pacific island nations threatened by sea level rise, say, "We are not drowning, we are fighting."

Back when I wrote *Hope in the Dark*, I was inspired by the Zapatistas, the indigenous visionaries who rose up in 1994 against 502 years of genocide continued by the Mexican government and the landowners in Chiapas. The Zapatistas were hopeful when, in 2019, twenty-five years into their revolution, they claimed eleven new territories, as is clear in the names they chose for two of them: "Esperanza de la Humanidad" (Hope of Humanity) and "Floreciendo la semilla rebelde" (The Rebellious Seed Blooms).

So was the Coalition of Immokalee Workers, a group of immigrant, often undocumented farmworkers in Florida, who fought battle after battle against major powers and won. They got better wages by winning campaigns against the largest fast-food and supermarket chains in the US; they fought modern-day slavery in the fields and sent the enslaving farm owners to prison; and they never stopped. Most people asked to bet on, say, undocumented farmworkers versus McDonald's would have put their money on the latter—and lost.

Proclaiming someone's or something's defeat contributes to it. It's a form of sabotage. This is as true of the climate movement, which is bedeviled by defeatists and doomsayers. I remember that we were never going to stop the Keystone XL pipeline—or so said the armchair experts, who, by discouraging participation, essentially campaigned for that outcome, because such speech is itself a form of participation. After more than a decade of organizing and activism, the death blow was delivered to KXL in 2021, but so many campaigns and the climate movement as a whole would be a lot easier without this disparagement, which serves as a brake when we need accelerators.

I regularly come across people who are not as engaged as climate activists or as informed as climate scientists, who confidently proclaim that no one cares, no one is doing anything, the problems are insoluble, the solutions don't exist or won't work, and often even some version of either "Life on Earth will soon terminate" or "We are all going to die." Sometimes these things are said by anxious and despondent people, and my heart goes out to them (and the nottoolateclimate.com project I run with Thelma Young Lutunatabua is for them), especially if they're young and just too deferential toward doomsayers and false prophets.

But sometimes powerful people seem to say it triumphantly and seem more eager to convince others than question their own assumptions or listen to the scientists. Not a few people—in particular, white men, it seems—confident in their own competence, write screeds of defeatism and doom. They often get basic facts wrong about the science, the solutions, the movement, and the popular will.

Others seem eager to deliver alarming news and unable to interpret complex data or sift for credibility competently, as with a Scottish newspaper that, in the spring of 2022, ran a front-page story misinterpreting one already dubious source to announce that the Atlantic Ocean was as good as dead. The article prompted a lot of shares and despair and grief on social media by people all too willing to defer to the presumed authority of a newspaper. I remain confounded that this is what some want to contribute to the public conversation; to me, it seems like bringing poison to the potluck.

A generalist in California wrote an editorial recently about how to address the fact that "Americans don't care about climate change," and while this might once have been the case, many recent studies show otherwise. Most Americans believe support for climate action is far lower than it really is, another obstacle to be overcome, and this editorialist was reinforcing that obstacle. In this particular case, the writer seemed simply uninformed, but others seem to see despair as an identity, a style, armor to put on before venturing out into the world.

To prophesy doom is to proclaim your own oracular powers. To take the stance of cynicism is to strive to seem worldly, to position yourself as someone who can't be fooled, though cynicism is often foolish about what is possible and how it all works. I have rarely seen people lambasted for being wrong in predicting defeat and destruction, while those who suggest that something positive might transpire are often mocked and scorned as soon as they open their mouths. Perhaps the scorners confuse being open to possibility with naivete, but in slamming the door on the latter locks out the former. Maybe it's all they believe is possible; maybe they love certainty more than possibility. Uncertainty brings its own anxiety, but it's one we must come to terms with, because it is the essential nature of the future.

Despair's cheerleaders offer the same message that institutions all around us do: that we are powerless, that power resides in the few, at the center, at the top. Part of resistance must consist of refusing to believe them, and that can be reinforced by better versions of history and theories of change. These can include the terror of the elites when ordinary people exercise their power. It's been on display from the late 1990s antiglobalization movement to 2011's Occupy Wall Street and Arab Spring to the George Floyd protests of 2020, as well as in response to the climate movement itself. And they can include the lessons of what began as unreasonable action. The New England women selling handsewn aprons at antislavery fundraisers in the 1840s could not reasonably see the end of slavery; a lone Swedish teenager protesting climate inaction could not reasonably expect her impact to be immense.

What motivates us to act is a sense of possibility within uncertainty—a sense that the outcome is not yet fully determined and our actions may matter in shaping it. This is all that hope is, and we are all teeming with it all the time in small ways. We plant a seed expecting both that it might grow and that we might be around to see it grow and admire the flower or eat the fruit. We buy five pounds of flour in the expectation we'll probably live long enough to do that much baking, buy a ticket for a trip weeks or months away. We may be run over by a bus on our way out for coffee in the morning, but we hope we'll be around to drink the whole cup and then get on with our day.

I've often tasted depression as hopelessness that the bleakness of the present will ever change, as those states of mind when nothing tastes good and nothing seems worthwhile and the obstacles to anything better seem insurmountable. Disciplines and routines have been one of my ways of keeping the gloom at bay, but I've also learned that the feeling that nothing will change is just mental weather, and that the record is all in favor of change (if not necessarily for the better). That's helped, too, and it's why I try to distinguish between despair as a feeling and as a forecast.

If we can recognize that we don't know what will happen, that the future does not yet exist but is being made in the present, then we can be moved to participate in making that future. We can be skillful enough to make directed efforts and sophisticated enough to know that results remain unpredictable. Many acts have had a huge positive impact, but not immediately or directly, so learning to look for and value slow and indirect consequences is crucial to recognizing the nature of change.

Uninformed and misplaced hope leads to fruitless effort and disappointment. One of the complexities of climate change activism is that there is much to hope for, but within the parameters of the possible—for example, we can, with swift and heroic effort, stabilize global temperature, scientists tell us, but that will not stop the ice sheets from melting and thus the seas from rising for centuries to come (though it will help with the pace and extent of that melting). We can campaign for proven solutions and not be taken in by the distractions, delaying tactics, and false solutions now being pushed by the same interests that once brought us climate denial. But what is possible is itself changing as technology and understanding evolve.

To hope is to risk. It's to take a chance on losing. It's also to take a chance on winning, and you can't win if you don't try (even though the campaign may be won without you). We who have materially safe and comfortable lives and who are part of societies and nations that contributed and still contribute the lion's share of greenhouse gases do not have the right to surrender on behalf of others. We have the obligation to act in solidarity with them. This begins by recognizing that the future has not yet been decided, because we are deciding it now.

On Not Meeting Nazis Halfway

When Trump won the 2016 election—while losing the popular vote—the *New York Times* seemed obsessed with running features about what Trump voters were feeling and thinking. These pieces treated them as both an exotic species and people it was our job to understand, understand being that word that means both to comprehend and to grant some sort of indulgence to. When Trump lost the 2020 election, the *Los Angeles Times* gave their editorial page over to letters from Trump voters, who had exactly the sort of predictable things to say that we have been hearing for years, thanks to the *New York Times* and what came to seem like about 11,000 other news outlets hanging on the every word of every white supremacist they could convince to go on the record.

The *Los Angeles Times* editor prefaced this feature with the declaration, "As one small attempt to bridge the divide, we are providing today a page full of letters from Trump supporters." The

This essay, published at lithub.com, was written in response to the widespread assertion by Democratic leaders and newspaper editorialists, immediately after the 2020 election, that we must now pander to the losers. It was written before the Republican campaign of lies led to the January 6, 2021, assault on the nation's Capitol as part of Trump's coup attempt.

implication is the usual one: we—urban multiethnic liberal-to-radical only-partly-Christian America—need to spend more time understanding MAGA America. The demands do not go the other way. Fox News and Ted Cruz and the Federalist Society have not urged their audiences, I feel pretty confident, to enter into discourse with, say, Black Lives Matter activists, radical rabbis, imams, abortion providers, undocumented valedictorians, or tenured lesbians. When only half the divide is being tasked with making the peace, there is no peace to be made, but there is a unilateral surrender on offer. We are told this is bipartisanship, but the very word means that both sides abandon their partisanship, and the right has absolutely no interest in doing that.

Paul Waldman wrote a valuable column in the *Washington Post* a few years ago, in which he pointed out that Democrats and progressives are routinely blamed for Republican and right-wing attitudes and conduct: "The assumption is that if Democrats simply choose to deploy this powerful tool of respect, then minds will be changed and votes will follow. This belief, widespread though it may be, is stunningly naive." He notes that the sense of being disrespected

> doesn't come from the policies advocated by the Democratic Party, and it doesn't come from the things Democratic politicians say. Where does it come from? An entire industry that's devoted to convincing white people that liberal elitists look down on them.... The right has a gigantic media apparatus that is devoted to convincing people that liberals disrespect them, plus a political party whose leaders all understand that that idea is key to their political project and so join in the chorus at every opportunity.

There's also often a devil's bargain buried in all this, the idea that you flatter and, yeah, respect these white people who think this country is theirs by throwing other people under the bus—by disrespecting immigrants and queer people and feminists and their rights and views. And you reinforce that constituency's sense that they matter more than other people when you pander like this, and pretty much all the problems we've faced over the past several years, to say nothing of the last five hundred, come from this sense of white people being more important than nonwhites, Christians than non-Christians, male than female, straight than queer, cisgender than trans.

Supreme Court Justice Samuel Alito complained that "you can't say that marriage is a union between one man and one woman. Now it's considered bigotry." This is a standard complaint of the right: the real victim is the racist who has been called a racist, not the victim of his racism; the real oppression is to be impeded in your freedom to oppress. And, of course, Alito is disingenuous; you *can* say that stuff against marriage equality (and he did). Then, other people can call you a bigot, because they get to have opinions, too, but in his scheme such dissent is intolerable, which is fun coming from a member of the party whose devotees wore "Fuck your feelings" shirts at its rallies and popularized the term "snowflake."

Nevertheless, we get this hopelessly naïve version of centrism, the idea that if we're nicer to the other side there will be no other side, just one big happy family. This inanity is also applied to the questions of belief and fact and principle, with some muddled cocktail of moral relativism and therapists' "everyone's feelings are valid" applied to everything. But the truth is not some compromise halfway between the truth and the lie, the fact and the delusion, the science and the propaganda. And the ethical is not halfway between white supremacists and human rights activists, rapists and feminists, synagogue massacrists and Jews, xenophobes and immigrants, delusional transphobes and trans people. Who the hell wants unity with Nazis until and unless they stop being Nazis?

Progressives genuinely have something to offer everyone, and we can and must win in the long run by offering it, offering it via better stories and better means to make those stories reach everyone. We actually want to see everyone have a living wage, access to health care, and lives unburdened by medical, student, and housing debt. We want this to be a thriving planet when the babies born this year turn eighty. But the popularly recommended compromise means abandoning and diluting our stories, not fortifying and improving them (and finding ways for them to actually reach the rest of America, rather than having them warped or shut out altogether).

Among the other problems with the *LA Times*'s editor's statement is that one side has a lot of things that do not deserve to be called facts, and their values too often advocate for harming many of us on the other side. Not to pick on one news outlet: on Sunday, November 15, 2020, the *Washington Post* ran a front-page subhead about the #millionMAGAmarch that read, "On stark display in the nation's capital were two irreconcilable versions of America, each refusing to accept what the other considered to be undeniable fact." Except that one side did have actual facts, notably that Donald J. Trump lost the election, and the other had hot and steamy delusions.

A lot of why the right doesn't "understand" climate change is that climate change tells us everything is connected, everything we do has far-reaching repercussions, and we're responsible for the whole, a message at odds with their idealization of a version of freedom that smells a lot like disconnection and irresponsibility. But, climate denial is also the result of fossil fuel companies and the politicians they bought spreading propaganda and lies for profit. If half of us believe the Earth is flat, we do not make peace by settling on it being halfway between round and flat. Those of us who know it's round will not recruit them through compromise. We all know that you do better at bringing people out of delusion by being kind and inviting than by mocking them, but that's inviting them to come over, which is not the same thing as heading in their direction.

The editor spoke of facts, and he spoke of values. In the past four years, too many members of the right have been emboldened to carry out those values as violence. One of the T-shirts at the #millionMAGAmarch: "Pinochet did nothing wrong." Except stage a coup, torture and disappear tens of thousands of Chileans, and violate laws and rights. A right-wing conspiracy to overthrow the Michigan government and kidnap governor Gretchen Whitmer was recently uncovered, racists shot some Black Lives Matter protesters and plowed their cars into a lot of protests this summer. The El Paso anti-immigrant massacre was only a year ago; the Pittsburgh synagogue massacre two years ago; the Charlottesville white-supremacist rally in which Heather Heyer was killed three years ago (and, of course, there have been innumerable smaller incidents all along). Do we need to bridge the divide between Nazis and non-Nazis? Because part of the problem is that we have an appeasement economy, a system that is supposed to be greased by being nice to the other side.

Appeasement didn't work in the 1930s, and it won't work now. That doesn't mean that people have to be angry or hostile or hate back, but it does mean they have to stand on principle and defend what's under attack. There are situations in which there is no common ground worth standing on, let alone hiking over to. If Nazis wanted to reach out and find common ground and understand us, they probably would not have had that tiki-torch parade in Charlottesville full of white men bellowing, "Jews will not replace us," and, also, they would not be Nazis. Being Nazis, white supremacists, misogynists, transphobes is all part of a project of refusing to understand as part of refusing to respect. It is a minority position, but by granting it deference we give it, over and over, the power of a majority position.

The whole Republican Party, since long before Trump, has committed itself to the antidemocratic project of trying to create a narrower electorate rather than win a wider vote. They have invested in voter suppression as a key tactic to win, and the votes they try to suppress are those of Black voters and other voters of color. That is a brutally corrupt refusal to allow those citizens the rights guaranteed to them by law. Having failed to prevent enough Black people from voting in the recent election, they are striving mightily to discard their votes after the fact. What do you do with people who think they matter more than other people? Catering to them reinforces the belief that they are more important, and their views must prevail. Deference to intolerance feeds intolerance.

Years ago, the linguist George Lakoff wrote that Democrats operate as kindly nurturance-oriented mothers to the citizenry, Republicans as stern discipline-oriented fathers. Another way to view the relationship between the two parties is as a marriage between an overly deferential wife and an overbearing and often abusive husband. *The Hill* just ran a headline that declared, "GOP Senators Say That a Warren nomination Would Divide Republicans." I am pretty sure they didn't run headlines that said, "Democratic Senators Say a Pompeo (or Bolton or Perdue or Sessions) Nomination Would Divide Democrats." I grew up in an era when wives who were beaten were expected to do more to soothe their husbands and not challenge them, and this carries on as the degrading politics of our abusive national marriage.

Some of us don't know how to win. Others can't believe they ever lost or will lose or should, and their intransigence constitutes a kind of threat. That's why the victors of the recent election are being told in countless ways to go grovel before the losers. This unilateral surrender is how misogyny and racism are baked into a lot of liberal and centrist as well as right-wing positions, this idea that some people need to be flattered and buffered even when they are harming the people who are supposed to do the flattering and buffering, even when they're breaking the law or lost the election. Lakoff didn't quite get to the point of saying that this nation is a household full of what domestic abuse advocates call coercive control, in which one partner's threats, intimidations, devaluations, and general shouting down control the other.

Feminism is good for everything, and it's a good model for seeing that this is both outrageous and a recipe for failure. It didn't work in marriages, and it was never the abused partner's job to prevent the abuse by surrendering ground and rights and voice. It is not working as national policy, either. Now is an excellent time to stand on principle and defend what we value, and I believe it's a winning strategy, too, or at least brings us closer to winning than surrender does. Also, it's worth repeating: *We won*, and being gracious in victory is still being victorious.

Against Centrism and Its Biases

The idea that all bias is some deviation from an unbiased center is itself a bias that prevents pundits, journalists, politicians, and plenty of others from recognizing some of the ugliest and most impactful prejudices and assumptions of our times. I think of this bias, which insists the center is not biased, not afflicted with agendas, prejudices, and destructive misperceptions, as status-quo bias. Underlying it is the belief that things are pretty okay now, that the people in charge should be trusted because power confers legitimacy, that those who want sweeping change are too loud or demanding or unreasonable, and that we should just all get along without looking at the skeletons in the closet and the stuff swept under the rug. It's mostly a prejudice of people for whom the system is working, against those for whom it's not.

I saw a tweet the other day that said the Secret Service and US Capitol police must have been incompetent or complicit to be blindsided by the January 6, 2021, insurrection. The writer didn't seem to grasp the third option: that the Secret Service was unable to see past the assumptions that middle-aged conservative white men don't pose a threat to democracy and the rule of law, that elected officials in powerful places weren't whipping up a riot or worse, that they assumed danger meant outsiders and others—them and not us. A decade ago, when I went to northern Japan for the first anniversary of the Great Tōhoku earthquake and tsunami, I was told that the hundred-foot-high wave of black water was so inconceivable a sight that some people could not recognize it and the danger it posed. Others assumed this tsunami would be no bigger than those in recent memory and did not flee to high enough ground. A lot of people died for not being able to see the unanticipated and unprecedented.

People fail to recognize things that do not fit into their worldview, which is why those in power have not adequately responded to decades of terrorism by white men—anti-reproductive-rights-driven killings, racial violence in churches, mosques, synagogues, and elsewhere; homophobia and transphobia; the misogynist violence behind a lot of mass shootings; attacks on environmentalists; and white supremacy in the ranks of the police and the military. US attorney general Merrick Garland finally called this terrorism by its true name and identified it as "the most dangerous threat to our democracy." The constant assumption has been that crime and trouble comes from outsiders, from "them," not "us," which is why the Black Lives Matter protests were constantly portrayed by conservatives and sometimes the mainstream as far more violent and destructive than they were, and why the right has had such an easy time demonizing immigrants.

What violence and destruction did take place in or adjacent to Black Lives Matter protests was often the work of the right. That includes the murder of a guard at a federal court in Oakland, allegedly by an air force sergeant and member of the Boogaloo Boys militia, while a BLM protest was going on nearby. It also reportedly includes some of the arson and vandalism in Minneapolis shortly after George Floyd's murder, as well as attacks on protesters, including the two fatal shootings in Kenosha, Wisconsin, by a right-wing teen. *USA Today* reported 104 such attacks by cars driven into crowds, most if not all of them apparently politically motivated. Police and opponents of the protests, in other words, committed serious violence, but their violence reinforced the status quo and was thereby not portrayed as menacing in the way that the phantasmagorical image of BLM protesters' violence was.

No one has ever loved the status quo more than the editorial board at the *New York Times*, which, in May 2021, composed an editorial declaring it a misstep for "the city's Pride organizers . . . to reduce the presence of law enforcement at the celebration, including a ban on uniformed police and corrections officers marching as groups until at least 2025." They found a lesbian of color who is also a cop and focused on this individual's feeling "devastated" rather than on the logic behind the decision. Pride celebrates the uprising against longtime police violence and criminalization of queerness at the Stonewall Bar in 1969. Police officers are in no way banned from participating out of uniform, if they so desire, but that's not enough for these "can't we all get along" editorialists, who also wrote: "But barring LGBTQ officers from marching is a politicized response and is hardly worthy of the important pursuit of justice for those persecuted by the police." You want to shout that the whole parade is political, because persecution and inequality have made being LGBTQ political, and the decision to include the police would be no less political than to exclude them. And who decides what's worthy? The idea that there is some magically apolitical state to which all should aspire is key to this bias and to why it refuses to recognize itself as a bias. It believes it speaks from neutral ground, which is why it forever describes a landscape of mountains and chasms as a level playing field.

The status-quo bias is something I've encountered over and over again in relation to gender violence, particularly as the refusal or inability to recognize that a high-status man or boy, be he film mogul or high-school football player, can also be a vicious criminal. Those who cannot believe the charges, no matter how credible, often instead dismiss and blame the victim (or worse: reporting a rape too often leads to death threats and other forms of harassment and intimidation intended to make an uncomfortable truth go away). Society has a marked failure of imagination when it comes to grasping that such predators treat their low-status victims in private spaces and moments differently than they treat their high-status peers in public. That failure of imagination denies the existence of such inequality even as it perpetrates it.

It's a failure born of undue respect for the powerful. Centrist bias is institutional bias, and all our institutions have historically perpetuated inequality. To deny it is to have it both ways—thinking yourself on the side of goodness while insisting no sweeping change is due. To recognize the pervasiveness of sexual abuse is to have to listen to children as well as adults, women as well as men, subordinates as well as bosses: it's to upend the old hierarchies of who should be heard and trusted, to break the silences that protect the legitimacy of the status quo. More than 95,000 people filed claims in the sexual-abuse lawsuit against the Boy Scouts of America, and what it took to keep all those children quiet while all those assaults took place is a lot of unwillingness to listen and to shatter faith in an institution that was itself so much part of the status quo (and, in many ways, an indoctrination system for it).

Centrists in the antebellum era were apathetic or outright resistant to ending slavery in the US and then, in the decades before 1920, to giving women the vote. The civil rights movement was not nearly as popular in its time as moderates who like the more polite quotes from Martin Luther King Jr think it was. King himself famously declared, "I have almost reached the regrettable conclusion that the Negro's great stumbling block in his stride toward freedom is not the White Citizen's Counciler or the Ku Klux Klanner, but the white moderate, who is more devoted to 'order' than to justice; who prefers a negative peace which is the absence of tension to a positive peace which is the presence of justice." As King notes, the status quo is always changing, and the centrists are often resistant to change that expands rights and justice, more mild about efforts by the right to shrink those things in favor of more inequality and more authoritarianism.

A recent study seems to contain the same biases, asserting, "We measured the brain activity of committed partisans watching real political video footage. Although all participants viewed the same videos, brain responses diverged between liberals and conservatives, reflecting differences in the subjective interpretation of the footage. This polarized perception was exacerbated by a personality trait: intolerance of uncertainty." The research seems to assume that many at either end of the spectrum hold strong beliefs and are intolerant of uncertainty, but who is more intolerant of uncertainty than those who want to believe that authority is trustworthy, no secrets need sunlight, and urgent cries for change are an annoyance?

Another fallacy of the centrist stance is that right and left are symmetrically extreme. Left-wing violence is largely a failed experiment that faded away in the 1970s. Also, in recent years the strongest voices on the left have mostly told important truths, whereas those on the right have promulgated lies while arguing against basic human rights. One obvious example is all the falsehoods about abortion used to justify undermining reproductive rights. Another is the conversation around the climate crisis. Progressives and scientists have been saying for a long time that we're in a dire situation that demands profound change. Yet, the call for change is painted as extreme—rather than as the necessary response to an extreme planetary crisis. On the right, the call has been for inaction and denial of the science. Only recently did the International Energy Agency get on board with what climate groups have been insisting on for years: an end to new fossil fuel exploration and extraction, a major shift now recognized as a reasonable and necessary one to preserve a livable planet.

Was it radical to be correct too soon? What gets called *the left* is often just ahead of the game when it comes to human rights and environmental justice; the right is often denying the existence of the problem, whether it's pesticides and toxic waste or domestic violence and child abuse. There is no symmetry. A lot of what are now considered moderate—aka centrist—positions were seen as radical not long ago, when this country supported segregation, banned interracial marriages and then same-sex marriages, prevented women from holding some positions and queer people from others, and excluded disabled people from almost everything. The center is biased, and those biases matter.

In the Shadow of Silicon Valley

Seeing cars with no human inside move through San Francisco's streets is eerie enough as a pedestrian, but when I'm on my bicycle I often find myself riding alongside them, and from that vantage point you catch the ghostly spectacle of a steering wheel turning without a hand. They are here despite opposition from city officials, including the fire chief, and San Francisco recently sued the California state bureau that gave companies license to use the streets as their laboratory. Firefighters have reported driverless cars attempting to park on firehoses; last June, one such car prevented emergency vehicles from reaching victims of a shooting. Direct communication isn't an option: the only way to get a driverless car to do anything is to contact the company in charge of it.

In early October 2023, a driverless car owned by Cruise, a subsidiary of General Motors, hit a woman who'd just been struck by another car, and in the course of performing what was described as a rote "pullover maneuver," dragged her twenty feet, mangling her badly and leaving her trapped under its wheels. The device was unable to detect that it was on top of a human and would not respond to rescuers, who had to lift the car off her. Cruise withdrew its 950 driverless vehicles, but Waymo, a company launched by Google's parent company, Alphabet, continues to send its cars onto the streets.

Driverless cars are often called autonomous vehicles—but driving isn't an autonomous activity. It's a cooperative social activity, in which part of the job of whoever's behind the wheel is to communicate with others on the road. Whether on foot, on my bike, or in a car, I engage in a lot of hand gestures—mostly meaning "Wait!" or "Go ahead!"—when I'm out and about, and I look for others' signals. San Francisco International Airport has signs telling people to make eye contact before they cross the street outside the terminals. There's no one in a driverless car to make eye contact with, to see you wave or hear you shout or signal back.

The rationales for the introduction of driverless cars include eliminating human error and allowing people with disabilities to get about without having to rely on other human beings. A more convincing rationale is that the corporations that own them can keep income that would otherwise have gone to drivers' wages. Automation has, of course, been a way to increase owners' profits since the Luddites protested against mechanical looms. Airports have self check-ins; supermarkets have self checkouts; roads and bridges have, in place of toll takers, technology that reads your license plate. Customer service phone numbers connect you to digital operatives and a host of other automated systems. We have lost dozens of points of human contact in our daily lives.

This takes a toll. Americans face a social pandemic of loneliness and isolation. The US surgeon general, Vivek Murthy, has declared it a crisis. His reports identify causes including the internet, smartphones, and social media. None of these was created with this agenda, but all of them have advanced it. Some of the "examples of harm" listed by Murthy include "technology that displaces in-person engagement, monopolizes our attention, reduces the quality of our interactions and even diminishes our self-esteem."

The Covid-19 pandemic worsened isolation, but tech had already made redundant many of the ways we used to congregate and mingle, while often portraying those ventures into the world as dangerous, unpleasant, inefficient, and inconvenient. There is an underlying assumption that each of us aspires to be as productive as possible and that stripping away everything that hinders productivity is a good thing. This was the pitch made by many new companies in the 1990s, when online shopping and other digital financial transactions first became a big deal. The shift has reshaped cityscapes as well as psyches. The American Booksellers Association reported that, in 2021 alone, "the movement of dollars to Amazon and away from retailers displaced 136,000 shops occupying 1.1 billion square feet of traditional commercial space." That's a lot of local jobs and relationships both to places and people.

The small independent businesses that we're losing sold goods, but they also gave away for free all sorts of things that are less tangible. There might be cheaper ways to buy shampoo or a better selection of envelopes online, but at an in-person store you can have a social interaction, even build a relationship with the proprietor and chat with other customers, or run into a friend or neighbor. That may happen in big chains such as Starbucks—but the employees aren't likely to be around for long, the profit doesn't go back into the community, and the design of the place is generic, not reflecting its locale. The exchanges between people who know one another are noncommodities these small businesses offer along with whatever is for sale.

In her urbanist manifesto *The Death and Life of Great American Cities* (1961), Jane Jacobs wrote about "eyes on the street": about the way that pedestrian traffic, people moving around—or sitting around—in public, kept a place safe and more than safe: convivial, gregarious. I think of what has come to my city as "the great withdrawal." People on the street often seem to have their eyes elsewhere, usually on their phones: they might video a crime, but they might also not notice it's happening. Many seem to flinch at direct contact with strangers or pretend the apparent intrusion didn't happen, so I've come to avoid the tiny interactions that seem much more welcome in New Orleans, even in New York City.

I moved to San Francisco in 1980, when street life and bar life were vibrant, but cafés were rare outside North Beach's Italian neighborhood. They proliferated in the 1980s and 1990s as places to hang out, maybe read, maybe chat to whomever was around, or just people-watch. In this millennium, in cafés frequented by young white people, every customer seems to be silently staring at an Apple product, so the places look and feel like offices. Even this phase may be on the way out.

The next phase—of trying to prevent customers from sticking around—has arrived. A food industry magazine published a story in April last year with the headline "In 2023, San Francisco Coffee Shops Want You to Get the Hell Out. The Vibe Is to Leave. Like Right Now," explaining that cafés were removing tables and chairs and focusing exclusively on take-away products, in part because cafés were being used as free office space. Cultural, social, and religious institutions have been displaced or run aground; film festivals and arts centers have left the city; theaters, thrift stores, and galleries have closed; historic businesses, including the oldest Black-owned bookstore in the US, have been evicted; all while wealth continues to concentrate at an extraordinary rate.

Though much of the late 1990s dotcom boom—and crash—happened in San Francisco, until about a dozen years ago Silicon Valley was generally thought of as San Jose, the city anchoring the south end of the Bay Area, and the suburban sprawl up the San Francisco peninsula. The luxury shuttle buses that Facebook, Google, and Apple launched around 2012 for their employees, by easing the congested commute, encouraged large numbers of them to move to San Francisco, which has now been fully annexed by the Valley. The desire of tech workers to live in this dense, diverse place while their products create its opposite is an ongoing conundrum. Many tech workers think of themselves as edgy, as outsiders, as countercultural, even as they're part of immense corporations that dominate culture, politics, and the economy. The much-told story of Apple's founding, in a garage near San Jose, doesn't change the fact that, with a market cap of $3 trillion, it's now the world's most valuable company.

Though the city has survived a series of local and national recessions in recent decades, San Francisco is said to be in a "doom loop" because so much office space and so many shops have been abandoned since the pandemic. Tech layoffs drove some of the shutdown, but the industry also enabled a mass white-collar withdrawal from the workplace—employees working from home, sometimes leaving the region to work remotely. More than the shrinkage of the population and the emptying out of downtown, the new mood of the city seems to be influenced by a kind of shrinking from human contact. The city remains the densely urban place it always was, but the way people inhabit it is increasingly suburban, looking to avoid strangers and surprises.

Over the past twenty years, ranks of glass towers have risen up just south of the city's old downtown. The second tallest building west of the Mississippi River is San Francisco's Salesforce Tower, whose resemblance, thanks to its curved sides and blunt edges, to a dildo or penis is often noted. It's certainly a monument to hubris. It's so tall that its isolated tip can be seen from many vantage points in the Bay Area—an Instagram account called @JustTheTipSF documents its intrusions. Completed in 2018, the tower has been half empty since Salesforce, with the volatility typical of the tech industry, laid off many of its employees early last year (before hiring another few thousand in the autumn). Tech companies routinely push out other businesses, only to flop or morph or migrate, leaving emptiness in their wake. Salesforce—the city's largest private employer—has also vacated Salesforce East, which stands next to yet another new high-rise, the mostly residential fifty-eight-story Millennium Tower, which opened in 2009. The marketing brochure for Millennium Tower called it the first "ultra-luxury high-rise . . . a sophisticated oasis in the heart of SoMa's tech capital," though, by 2015, its faulty construction had led to tilting and sinking. Following lawsuits from residents, $100 million was spent in an attempt to shore it up.

News stories in recent years have often described San Francisco as a cauldron of crime and depravity, held up as proof that progressive policies don't work. In recent years, right-wing media have propagated stories about crime, homelessness, and the city's real (but hardly unique) fentanyl crisis. On a TV debate in November between former mayor Gavin Newsom (now governor of California) and Ron DeSantis (far-right governor of Florida and failed candidate for the Republican nomination for president), DeSantis brandished a (made-up) map of human excrement in San Francisco that was supposed to clinch his arguments. It's a narrative that conservatives, including many tech barons, use to justify their demands for the kind of war on crime—more cops, harsher punishments, fewer civil liberties—that their predecessors pushed in the 1980s and 1990s.

Levels of violent crime are actually lower in San Francisco than in many American cities (and are far lower than they were here in the 1980s). Theft, including car break-ins and shoplifting, is also treated as dramatic, alarming, and a sign of social breakdown. A video of an impoverished-looking Black guy in a San Francisco drugstore stuffing a trash bag full of goods and wheeling it away on his bicycle became an online sensation in 2021. The closures of several downtown chain stores were blamed by their parent corporations on shoplifting, but when journalists looked into the stories, they found that in most cases outlets were closed because of low revenue and other more mundane problems.

Nevertheless, that San Francisco is in the grip of lawlessness is widely asserted. When the well-known tech executive Bob Lee (Google, Square, MobileCoin) was found fatally stabbed on the street in the early hours of April 4, 2023, many claimed that his murder was part of a crime wave by an out-of-control underclass. Elon Musk tweeted that "violent crime in SF is horrific and even if attackers are caught, they are often released immediately," implying that the culprit was a habitual criminal benefiting from lenient policies. The tech venture capitalist Matt Ocko raged: "Chesa Boudin [the former San Francisco district attorney] & the criminal-loving city council that enabled him and a lawless SF for years have Bob's literal blood on their hands."

But, it turned out that the man charged with Lee's murder, Nima Momeni, was a fellow tech entrepreneur who had been with Lee that evening. Lee died with cocaine and ketamine in his system; local news reported that the victim, the alleged murderer, and the murderer's sister had all been doing drugs that day. At least some of the drugs seem to have come from Jeremy Boivin, a friend of Lee's, also previously in tech, who was arrested in 2021, with a kilo of cocaine and a kilo of methamphetamine, and again in 2022, for possession of cocaine, heroin, and meth. In 2020, he was charged with giving the date-rape drug GHB to his housekeeper and sexually assaulting her (according to *Rolling Stone*, Lee paid his bail). The district attorney who prosecuted Boivin, Chesa Boudin, noted that there is a belief "among conservatives in this city that it's only scary poor people who are doing drugs. The reality is that the tech industry is deep in . . . drugs." The city's main online news site, Mission Local, quoted a friend of Momeni's, who said that he had a cocaine problem of "the regular Bay Area executive sort." Momeni's attorneys suggested the murderer might be a homeless man who was found sleeping near where Lee died, even though Momeni's DNA was found on the handle of the murder weapon, a kitchen knife that matched a set in his sister's kitchen.

A security camera captured Lee and Momeni leaving the Millennium Tower, where Momeni's sister lived with her plastic surgeon husband. They got into Momeni's white BMW; another security camera caught them getting out of the car a few blocks away. For a moment they are hidden; then Momeni can be seen getting back into the car and driving away. Lee, staggering into view of yet another security camera, managed to call 911 to report that he'd been stabbed. He was found bleeding and unconscious on the sidewalk and was pronounced dead at the hospital.

Lee collapsed in front of a luxury apartment building at 403 Main Street. The address seemed familiar, so I looked it up: it's a block from the 301 Main Street Infinity Tower, in whose $7 million penthouse the tech mogul Gurbaksh Chahal was, a decade earlier, recorded on his own bedroom surveillance camera clobbering a woman 117 times and repeatedly threatening to kill her. He was dumped as CEO of his ad-tech firm and eventually did prison time for violating his probation with another round of violence against another woman. Chahal currently heads a startup whose actual functions are wreathed in the flowery vagueness—"cutting-edge AI seamlessly merges with global commerce . . . shifting from basic transactions to insightful exchanges"—endemic to industry prose.

Crime in the San Francisco Bay Area can be described in many ways. But there are no dramatic videos showing Palo Alto native son turned crypto mogul Sam Bankman-Fried misappropriating $8.6 billion of clients' money, or of the scam run by ex-Stanford student Elizabeth Holmes, who raised $700 million for Theranos, a company whose sole product was a medical technology that didn't exist. Holmes, who used to live in a $15 million mansion and fly in a private Theranos jet, is doing time in federal prison for defrauding investors. Bankman-Fried was sentenced to twenty-five years and ordered to pay $11 billion in forfeiture. Those thefts were crimes in the most traditional sense, but the sheer wealth generated by Silicon Valley has given its pack of billionaires the belief that they are above or beyond the law. Most of them made their fortunes in finance or technology; those fortunes and the accompanying hubris and seclusion convinced them they were magnificent at everything and anything, including remaking society according to their lights.

In 2022, the billionaires David Sacks, former COO of PayPal, and William Oberndorf pumped money into a successful recall campaign against Boudin, shortly after his election as district attorney (accused of being soft on crime, Boudin was the DA prosecuting Bob Lee's drug dealer). A total of $7 million was donated to the effort, 80 percent of it in amounts of $50,000 or more, $600,000 from Oberndorf alone; he has also spent extravagantly to back charter schools and fight the teachers' union. Sacks, a friend of Musk's, is a major backer of right-wing candidates for national office and seemingly obsessed with urban crime. Another tech/venture capital billionaire and opponent of Boudin, Ron Conway, has long used his wealth to push San Francisco to the right. In 2010, he was a driving force behind an ordinance banning sitting on the sidewalk, intended to criminalize those with nowhere else to go. In 2016, Conway and Oberndorf funded a ballot proposition to outlaw tent encampments, the homes of last resort for the unhoused. The tech elite tends to regard the homeless not as people with unmet needs but as an intrusion or even assault on the sensibilities of others. If you equate your wealth with virtue, you tend to equate poverty with vice, and the enemies of the homeless routinely portray them as criminals. The assumption that Bob Lee was murdered by the underclass rather than one of his own speaks to this, as well as to the sense among tech leaders that they are the heroes, the people with solutions, sometimes the victims, but never the villains.

Perhaps the existence of the unhoused, stranded in an outside with no inside to retreat to, along with tech's offerings and ideology, has encouraged people to stay indoors or to venture into public spaces only with reluctance or trepidation. The proliferation of delivery services has made eating restaurant food at home common. "The exploitation economy is just as unhealthy and dehumanizing for the customers as it is for the workers," Andrew Callaway, a San Francisco gig worker, wrote in 2016. "You never even have to see the person who is cleaning your house or your clothes. Plenty of people requested that I drop off their food at the door. Customers grow to love apps that make the worker anonymous." In this system, the invisible hand of the market can actually bring you a burrito.

By producing such extremes of wealth, tech is returning us to a kind of feudalism, with a few powerful figures accountable to no one. Here's Elon Musk, the world's richest person, who—after buying Twitter for an inflated $44 billion—invited in misinformation, disinformation, and hate, providing a platform for extreme right-wingers, racists, and conspiracy theorists, while also using his Starlink satellite technology first for and then against the Ukrainian military in their conflict with Russia. "There is little precedent for a civilian's becoming the arbiter of a war between nations," Ronan

Farrow wrote in the *New Yorker*, "or for the degree of dependency that the US now has on Musk in a variety of fields, from the future of energy and transportation to the exploration of space." Farrow also reported that people who know Musk say that his ketamine use "has escalated in recent years, and that the drug, along with his isolation and his increasingly embattled relationship with the press, might contribute to his tendency to make chaotic and impulsive statements and decisions."

Here's Mark Zuckerberg, the fifth richest, who has turned a blind eye to Facebook's role in election corruption around the world and in the genocide in Myanmar, and to Instagram's role in the teenage mental health crisis. His company recently lost $46 billion on the Metaverse, the virtual-reality venture he has earnestly promoted. "Pretty soon," he said in September 2022, "we're going to be at a point where you're going to be there physically with some of your friends, and others will be there digitally as avatars or holograms, and they'll feel just as present as everyone else." Like technocrats before him, Zuckerberg insists that online connection is a perfect substitute for human contact.

Here's Peter Thiel, founder of PayPal, who put $10 million into the lawsuit that in 2016 bankrupted the website Gawker, which had earlier outed him as gay. This might make you think he cared about privacy, but he also founded Palantir, which surveils immigrants for the Department of Homeland Security, assisted in Cambridge Analytica's weaponization of Facebook user data on Trump's behalf, and, according to the Intercept, "has helped expand and accelerate the NSA's global spy network, which is jointly administered with allied foreign agencies around the world." Big tech is ferociously protective of its own privacy while abusing ours. Frank Wilhoit's claim that "conservatism consists of one proposition: there must be in-groups whom the law protects but does not bind, alongside out-groups whom the law binds but does not protect" applies precisely to the industry and its captains.

While Musk dreams of space travel and colonies on other planets, Thiel dreams of immortality. Many tech billionaires do not believe they should be bound by the laws of nations or biology, and apparently want to continue consuming an outsize amount of the world's resources indefinitely. "I stand against confiscatory taxes, totalitarian collectives and the ideology of the inevitability of the death of every individual," Thiel wrote in an online libertarian journal in 2009. "I no longer believe that freedom and democracy are compatible." He didn't choose democracy.

For a while, Thiel backed the libertarian wet dream known as seasteading, building artificial islands beyond government control. Thiel's attempt to build a postapocalyptic bunker in a remote part of New Zealand's South Island was rejected, but Bill Gates, now only the world's eighth richest person, has his own island in Belize. Oracle's Larry Ellison, the world's fourth richest person, owns 98 percent of the Hawaiian island of Lanai, resort hotels and all, which he's made an inhospitable place for anyone who's not enormously wealthy. Larry Page, who cofounded Google and is right behind Gates in the wealth rankings, owns five islands outright, including isolated spots off Fiji, Puerto Rico, and the Virgin Islands. According to *Wired*, Zuckerberg's private compound, covering 1,400 acres of the Hawaiian island of Kauai, includes multiple mansions and luxury treehouses, plus an underground bunker. (Tech billionaires often seem more interested in surviving the apocalypse than preventing it.) Nondisclosure agreements bind the construction workers who built it, and a long wall shuts off other islanders from any view of the sea while making access to the public beach extremely difficult.

You can't really be in favor of both democracy and billionaires, because democracy requires equal opportunity in order to participate, and extreme wealth gives its holders unfathomable advantages with little accountability. I've long believed that democracy depends in part on coexisting with strangers and people unlike you, and feeling that you have something in common with them. The internet has helped people withdraw from diverse communities, public and communal spaces, and shared experiences to huddle in like-minded online groups, including groups focused on hating those they see as unlike them, while encouraging the disinhibition of anonymity.

Sometimes disconnection is itself the business model, as with San Francisco–based Airbnb, which has undermined neighborhoods around the world, from major cities to rural communities, by turning long-term housing, where people had roots and relationships, into short-term rentals, often jacking up the price of housing at the same time. A friend of mine who lives in Joshua Tree, the semirural community in the desert east of Los Angeles, has found herself surrounded entirely by short-term rentals, so she no longer has neighbors in the usual sense of the word.

The choices tech titans make in their personal lives—gated communities, private schools, private jets, megayachts, private islands—show that a segregated, shrouded life is their ideal, as it generally is for the superrich. But they profit off technologies that, while encouraging our own social withdrawal, are focused on capturing as much information about us as possible. That is, we are both more isolated and less private than we've ever been. I have never to my knowledge seen any of these billionaires, but by necessity I use their platforms and software and move among their employees. I live in a city and to some extent in a world that has been radically reshaped by their urges and ideals, which are not my urges and ideals.

In an essay for the *New Republic* in 2022 about Sacks and his isolationist, new-right peers, Jacob Silverman wrote, "These frightened urbanites are echoing the Trumpist drumbeat that cities—particularly in California—are dangerous, dark places that must be tamed." But they never really loved San Francisco, at least not as a place of diversity and free circulation, and they've never acknowledged their role in its dramatic economic divides, housing crises, and desperate homeless population.

A group of these disgruntled tycoons has, however, decided to build a new city on the northeastern outskirts of the Bay Area. Flannery Associates—a billionaires' consortium whose members include Laurene Powell Jobs (Steve Jobs's widow), Reid Hoffman (cofounder of LinkedIn), and the venture capitalists Marc Andreessen and Michael Moritz—quietly bought up fifty thousand acres of farmland in Solano County at a cost of around $800 million. (By way of comparison, San Francisco covers about thirty thousand acres.) The area's representative in Congress, John Garamendi, told the *Los Angeles Times* that "Flannery Associates is using secrecy, bullying and mobster tactics to force generational farm families to sell."

Last August, the group revealed its hand, sending out a survey announcing its intention to build "a new city with tens of thousands of new homes, a large solar energy farm, orchards with over a million new trees, and over ten thousand acres of new parks and open space." Its website doesn't give real answers to questions about the environmental impact of such a massive development, about the governance of a new city founded and (presumably) owned by an elite, about the public services needed for this private enterprise. Instead, Flannery Associates has released sedate pastel-toned pictures of blank-faced children playing on tree-lined streets of quaint row houses and blank-faced adults with brown and black as well as white skin riding bikes and sitting in a plaza.

It seems unlikely that any of the associates want to live in those row houses themselves or send their children out to play on the street or ride the train with the Black lady in the picture. In 2022, Andreessen and his wife inveighed against building multifamily housing in their swanky Peninsula hometown of Atherton—average annual income $539,000, median home price $7.9 million—with an email to city government that read: "Please immediately remove all multifamily overlay zoning projects from the Housing Element which will be submitted to the state in July. They will massively decrease our home values, the quality of life of ourselves and our neighbors and immensely increase the noise pollution and traffic." People who live in apartments, never mind tents, were scum they didn't want around, housing crisis be damned.

In a way, ultrarich people don't live anywhere: they are nomads who circulate between multiple dwellings. Andreessen owns a $177 million compound in Malibu, and Jobs has three mansions there, along with palatial homes in San Francisco and Palo Alto, a rural retreat in Los Altos Hills near San Jose, an equestrian estate in Florida, a fifteen-thousand-square-foot home in Woodside (the rural district of choice for Silicon Valley's richest), and part of Kona Village, a Hawaiian resort.

Local opposition to the Flannery Associates project has been ferocious, and the county government responded by declaring that it wouldn't rezone farmland for urban development. I don't know whether these billionaires know what a city is, but I do know that they have laid their hands on the city that's been my home since 1980 and used their wealth to undermine its diversity and affordability, demonize its poor, turn its politicians into puppets, and push its politics to the right. They have produced many kinds of dystopia without ever deviating from the line that they are bringing us all to a glorious utopia for which they deserve our admiration.

I used to be proud of being from the San Francisco Bay Area. I thought of this place in terms of liberation and protection; we were where the environmental movement was born; we were the land of experimental poetry and antiwar marches, of Harvey Milk and gay rights, of the occupation of Alcatraz Island that galvanized a nationwide Indigenous rights movement as well as Cesar Chavez's farmworkers' movement in San Jose and the Black Panthers in Oakland. We were the left edge of America, a refuge from some of its brutalities and conformities, a sanctuary for dissidents and misfits, and a laboratory for new ideas. We're still that lab, but we're no longer an edge; we're a global power center, and what issues from here—including a new superelite—shapes the world in increasingly disturbing ways.

Masculinity as Radical Selfishness

I grew up with the old axiom "My right to swing my arm ends where your nose begins," which is about balancing personal freedom with the rights of others and one's own obligation to watch out for those rights. The maliciously gendered rhetoric of the National Rifle Association, the incel and pick-up artist subcultures, Trumpism, and a lot else have proposed, in recent years, that, actually, their right to swing their arms doesn't end, and my nose and your nose are not their problem or are just in the way and need to move.

Wearing masks, it turns out, is not manly, when the definition of manly is not having to do fuck-all out of concern for others. There are a lot of other things that turn out not to be manly, including, according to recent studies, caring about climate change and environmental problems, and even recycling and handwashing. Taking care of things is not manly. Four of the worst-hit countries in the pandemic are also afflicted with heads of state preoccupied with meeting the terms of machismo—Brazil's Bolsonaro, Russia's Putin, the UK's Boris Johnson, the US's Trump—in ways that con-

---

Written in May 2020, early in the Covid-19 pandemic shutdown.

Masculinity as Radical Selfishness

flict with recognizing the gravity of the Covid-19 crisis and responding adequately.

This is a definition of masculinity as radical selfishness, and just as it's taken a huge toll in American lives by demanding and utilizing deregulation of access to semiautomatic weapons and other implements of mass death, so has it taken a huge toll by insisting that we don't have to respond to the pandemic because the "we" that is not responding imagines itself as invulnerable and full of unlimited arm-swinging rights. As the conservative philosophy intent on cutting taxes and social services and safety regulations, it's been making inroads for decades.

In the US, unlimited arm-swinging peaks at an intersection between whiteness and maleness, with plenty of white women on board who seem to believe that a white lady's job is to protect white men's arm-swinging (often with a selfless disregard for their own noses). The logic behind all this stuff is that the isolated individual—ideally white, ideally male; they are the fists; the rest are inconvenient noses—must rule supreme. But, as it turns out, radical self-reliance ends where social withdrawal actually begins to be a form of care for others in this pandemic. Thus, the white men who had been telling us all along that they are rugged commandos of self-sufficiency who could live alone in the postapocalyptic woods off what they could hunt with their bare hands suddenly declared they needed help right away with their hair.

At the other end of the spectrum were women making masks so that vulnerable populations and frontline workers had a better chance of surviving this thing. Caregiving has been gendered as feminine and so has sewing, and though I have seen men making masks, I have seen a lot more women doing this, many of them I've kept tabs on sewing steadily day after day. This is the extreme antithesis of too-manly-to-wear-a-mask syndrome. It's not just caring enough to do the no-real-work of wearing a mask; it's caring enough to do the huge work of trying to see that everyone has a mask, and so, all over America, are (mostly) women sewing for strangers.

It's nurturance work and protective work. Mega-masculinity only likes the idea of protection if it's in the action hero mode of protecting something by blowing something else away. Meanwhile, we are being told that the stay-at-home decrees in the US have meant, for that peculiarly popular arrangement that is heterosexual two-parent families, that women are doing most of the work. Many academic outlets note that women's scholarly productivity, measured as submissions to scholarly journals, have fallen off during the pandemic, while men's have stayed steady or risen. This is, as the journal *Nature* put it, because "women scholars may be more likely to face an intensification of domestic responsibilities when confined to the home and, consequently, a reduction in scholarly production."

You could rewrite that sentence as "men scholars may be less likely to take responsibility at home and to experience, as a result, reduction in professional impact." But we always tell these stories as being about women, as being stuff that somehow happens to women and that women need to address. One way this happens is by segregating articles about such things in women's sections of publications. Women's sections in newspapers and magazines have always annoyed me, because they too often make concerns that should be everyone's into women's concerns and women's work to fix.

The *Washington Post* has a section called The Lily, a name clearly designed to funnel women in and filter men out. A recent story there bore the headline, "'I Had to Choose Being a Mother': With No Child Care or Summer Camps, Women Are Being Edged Out of the Workforce." Subtitle: "When Parents Can't Do It All, Women's Paid Labor Is Often the First to Go." Its very placement says, "This happens to women; this is a woman's problem." We've had the story told this way about so many things. Changing the grammar would change whose responsibility it is to do something about it, or to stop doing it, and so does changing who's the subject of the story.

I wanted to retitle this Lily story and put it where men would see it, or see someone write a story for them, about them, with interviews about the decisions they made, and how they benefited from them. With headlines like, "I Chose Not to Coparent Equally and Helped Edge My Wife Out of the Workforce" or "How to Unwittingly Ruin a Marriage and a Career at the Same Time by Being a Selfish Jerk." Maybe in the spirit of peppy women's sections, a men's section piece titled, "Strategic Obliviousness Is How I Perpetuate Patriarchy, and I Bet You Do Too!" Maybe we got it in the *New York Times*, on May 8, 2020: "Nearly Half of Men Say They Do Most of the Home Schooling. 3 Percent of Women Agree."

The feature in The Lily frames childcare as a thing women need, which assumes that it's women's responsibility and maybe something men give to women, rather than that every parent ought to care for their offspring. It focuses on a woman with a demanding career and a stay-at-home husband, who had to quit her job because he wouldn't do jack and claimed, with what's often labeled "learned helplessness" but could be called strategic helplessness, that he couldn't. "But could she ask her husband to handle 12-hour shifts of child care, with no help, no breaks and no clear end point? She wasn't sure her family could survive that. She wasn't sure he'd do it, even if she asked." Why does one (working) parent have to ask the other (nonworking) one to parent? Why is doing what literally billions of women do day after day framed as some terrible ordeal? Where is the headline, "Local Man Cannot Parent

Own Child"?

The Hawai'i State Commission on the Status of Women issued, in April 2020, *A Feminist Economic Recovery Plan for COVID-19*, which says some of this beautifully:

> Caregiving, associated with and expected of women, is necessary for economic production to take place and yet it is split off from economic production, thereby structurally subordinating women in society. This is why even within their own racial, indigenous status, and economic groups, women are the most marginalized. Case in point: Native Hawaiian women are more economically vulnerable than Native Hawaiian men, earning 70 cents for every dollar a man makes, and 79 cents for every dollar a Native Hawaiian man makes. Women will never be able to equally participate in Hawai'i's economy without a social care infrastructure and if men are not supported and incentivized to share care activities.

All of which is to say, we had a pandemic, and it was experienced unequally along race and class lines, and it also intersected with what maybe we should call the pandemic of patriarchy, which made it far worse by action and inaction that amplified the spread and impact of the disease and punished women in the ways it always punishes women, through violence and the shifting of the responsibility of caregiving onto them.

Which intersects with the malignancy of whiteness, when it is white people threateningly demanding unlimited freedoms in a pandemic that, here in the US, disproportionately kills Black and brown people.* The good news is that, unlike Covid-19, we know

---

* After this was written, as Covid vaccines became available and refusing them became part of right-wing culture, the demographics of who was dying

what the cure is for the gender part. The short version is: feminism. Now, in size XXL, for men. And the rest: feminism is just a subset of human rights, and universal human rights and absolute equality would answer all those questions about what to do about coronavirus and nearly everything else.

---

shifted a lot, toward white people.

Abortion Is an Economic Issue

Being a parent is expensive. Being a criminal is also expensive, whether you lose economic opportunities to avoid apprehension or spend money on your defense if apprehended or go to prison and lose everything and, marked as a felon, emerge unemployable. Abortion is an economic issue, because when it's not legal, those are the two remaining options, leaving out being dead, which you could argue is either very expensive or absolutely beyond the realm of money. Being dead is also on the table because women have all too often died from lack of access to reproductive health care, including abortions (to say nothing of being unable to leave an abuser, to whom pregnancy and children can bind you more tightly). Widespread abortion bans mean they are facing more of that now.

Having no options but to be dead, a criminal, or a parent is not a sane or moral argument for parenthood, and it's also pretty different from having certain inalienable rights, including life, liberty, and the pursuit of happiness. Also, now that abortion is unavailable under almost all circumstances in Texas and other states, it's an economic justice issue in that those with the financial capacity to take time off, travel in search of care, and pay for it out of pocket are not affected the way those who cannot do so are. And those who can afford to get an abortion under these circumstances are also those who can afford to defend themselves against possible criminal charges.

All of which is to say, abortion is an economic issue and a labor issue, as well as a human rights and health care issue, as the AFL-CIO and other labor unions have recognized. So, it's been confounding to see some supposedly progressive men say that people should talk about economics instead of abortion, as if the loss of reproductive rights isn't a huge economic blow to anyone facing the possibility of an unwanted pregnancy.

Access to birth control and abortion laid the groundwork for US women to begin to claim financial, professional, and educational equality—a goal still far from realized, overall, but reproductive rights sanded down the mountains and filled in the chasms a little. Taking that away pushes women back into the grim era when an unplanned, unwanted pregnancy could upend a life, stop an education, stymie a career, force unwanted dependency on the person who caused that pregnancy—an era when self-determination was an aspiration, not a given.

The *Dobbs* decision, striking down *Roe v. Wade* on June 24, 2022, was cavalier about all this. The majority opinion pretends that bearing a child no longer has significant social and economic impact. It cites, among its justifications, that

> attitudes about the pregnancy of unmarried women have changed drastically; that federal and state laws ban discrimination on the basis of pregnancy; that leave for pregnancy and childbirth are now guaranteed by law in many cases; that the costs of medical care associated with pregnancy are covered by insurance or government assistance;

that states have increasingly adopted 'safe haven' laws, which generally allow women to drop off babies anonymously; and that a woman who puts her newborn up for adoption today has little reason to fear that the baby will not find a suitable home.

In other words, there is no reason not to have an unplanned or unwanted child; doing so is no big deal.

Those are callous lies. The right not to bear children isn't just about respectability for the unmarried, and to frame it that way while ignoring the profound and lasting emotional, psychological, physical, moral, and financial impact of carrying a pregnancy for nine months and giving birth is outrageous. Discrimination against people who may get pregnant or are pregnant continues despite those laws; many pregnant people continue to lack access to health care; and the fact that a baby can be handed over is no justification for being forced to bear it. Furthermore, as another branch of the US government that the Supreme Court could have consulted reports: "The number of children waiting to be adopted also fell in fiscal year 2020 to 117,000"; the number in foster care was more than 400,000.

One of the striking things about discussions in defense of abortion rights in recent months is the testimony by those who've undergone pregnancy, miscarriage, and childbirth about how physically grueling and even life-threatening those experiences can be. Pregnancy can incapacitate women for months, which is obviously economically devastating to a poor person working in the gig economy or, say, in a nail salon or a fast-food restaurant. It can be an overwhelming experience, interfering particularly with the ability to perform physical labor: the judge may be able to toil on when the janitor cannot. A lot of people make a living through work that is physically demanding (and does not include benefits such as sick leave and parental leave).

Also, we need to stop defining abortion as a stand-alone right and look at the criminalization of pregnancy and motherhood, especially for poor and nonwhite women. "More than 50 women have been prosecuted for child neglect or manslaughter in the United States since 1999 because they tested positive for drug use after a miscarriage or stillbirth," reported the Marshall Project, while noting that miscarriages are common under all circumstances. "Sentences have ranged from probation to 20 years in prison. . . . Women prosecuted after pregnancy loss are often those least able to defend themselves, the investigation found. They typically work low-paying jobs, are often victims of domestic abuse, have little access to health care or drug treatment, and rely on court-appointed lawyers who advise them that pleading guilty is their best option." Too, some women die from pregnancy and childbirth, and thanks to unequal medical care, Black women have the highest incidence of such deaths. Pregnancy and childbirth can also cause permanent physical changes, including lasting pain and disability.

The laws making the most intimate conditions of a body and life subject to legal intrusion are reportedly already preventing pregnant people from seeking health care and spreading well-founded fear. Making the administration of an abortion a crime is frightening medical caregivers and interfering with their ability to provide care. Some of the proposed abortion bans would include life-saving abortions, and we have already seen cases in which medical care was withheld until a woman's life was actively in danger. Women are already being denied prescriptions when those drugs can be used in abortions, another way that taking away abortion rights is turning into a broader loss of rights.

The financial and professional impact of parenting in heterosexual relationships still mostly falls on women. The majority of women who have abortions are already mothers raising kids; we are in a childcare crisis that has, along with the long months schools were shut during the pandemic, crushed a lot of women's working lives and financial independence. As Congresswoman Alexandria Ocasio-Cortez noted in late September 2022, "When the powerful force people to give birth against their will, they trap millions in cycles of economic setback and desperation. Especially in a country without guaranteed health care. And desperate workers are easier to exploit." The Supreme Court majority pretended it was undermining access to reproductive rights because they have no significant impact, but of course the court's agenda was the opposite: to impose the conditions that make women subordinate in rights and economic status.

Postscript: Written shortly after the Supreme Court's overturning of *Roe v. Wade* in June 2022, this essay anticipated that women would die for lack of care. Since then, women have died, in Georgia, Indiana, and Texas. There have been many horrific reports of people whose miscarriages need immediate medical care being left to wait until medical caregivers, intimidated by fear of prosecution under new state laws, deem intervention to be "life-saving." That means the patient has gone septic, lost massive amounts of blood, or is otherwise near death because of the denial or delay of care. Obstetrician-gynecologists and other doctors are also reportedly leaving states with these restrictive laws, notably Idaho, thereby impacting the pregnant in yet other ways. While the number of deaths is relatively small, the threat to the pregnant means that the impact is huge. (Meanwhile, attacks on trans people sometimes manifest as an insistence that trans men are giving up their ability to bear children—which is in many cases not true—and an assertion that one's fertility is other people's business.)

Toward a Democracy of Voices

When I was young, I had no words. I read voraciously, I loved books, stories, language. I was trying to become a writer, and so I lived for words and by words. I poured out my thoughts and some of the hopes and fears that were beginning to take shape in long conversations with friends. But words failed me when I needed them most.

I was a young woman in the 1980s, long before all the contemporary conversations about consent and believing victims began, before terms like acquaintance rape and workplace sexual harassment were in regular circulation. I lived in a time when it seemed so unlikely that the men who menaced me on the street and sometimes elsewhere would respect my words if I said, *No, leave me alone, I'm not interested*, that I despaired beforehand and tried instead to slip away, evade, dodge, shrink, disappear.

I was mute in those moments. I knew that speaking was more likely to make things worse than better for me, though women in the situations I found myself in were often rebuked for not speaking up. The pleasant story behind that rebuke was that we were all equal rational beings, and we all had the power of language at our command, and anyone who didn't use it chose not to, and it was all on her.

That was a lie. We did not have equal power. Sometimes saying *no* or *stop* achieved nothing. Sometimes speaking up further enraged the man we were trying to escape. Some of us, many of us, millions of us were sexually assaulted and then told we were liars when we spoke of what happened, and so our society was able to pretend it cared about sexual harassment and assault while refusing to acknowledge their omnipresence. We do things with words when they have power—set boundaries, swear oaths, bear witness. But if your words have no power, it is almost worse to speak them than not, to see them fail than not.

Facts circulate freely in a democracy of information that results from a democracy of voices. We have something else instead, from personal life to national politics: a hierarchy of audibility and credibility, a brutal hierarchy in which people with facts often cannot prevail, because those who have more power push those facts out of the room and into silence or make the cost of stating those facts dangerously high. That's how the oil industry turned the science of climate change into a fake debate full of fake uncertainties. And it's how Harvey Weinstein raised an army to protect his power to grab and grope and rape with impunity for decades. Sexual assault is perhaps the grimmest and clearest example of how unequal power generates crimes and then protects those who create them, but it's not the only one.

The story of Weinstein and his army of aggressive protectors has been exemplary of this. More than ninety women reported that he harassed or assaulted them, but Mr. Weinstein had what money can buy: an international army of lawyers, spies, influencers, and others toiling to control the story and keep his secrets. That is, to silence and discredit the women he assaulted. Which means that so many of them were subjected to a double silencing. The first time was when they were sexually assaulted—an act that is about disregard for someone's right to determine what does and does not happen to them, to have a voice in what happens. ("If he heard the word 'no,' it was like a trigger for him," said one of the women who testified that he raped her.) The second silencing was when they were intimidated out of speaking up or paid to be silent or threatened with or actually had their reputations or their careers ruined, or some combination of those things.

Weinstein's trial was widely covered, so we finally heard some of the victims—but this is not just about exceptionally powerful men and young women in an industry that makes headlines. There are countless stories of silencing elsewhere every day. Most of these stories don't make the news at all. Other times the news is saturated with them—the other day, Weinstein, Trump, Julian Assange, the Jeffrey Epstein backer and Victoria's Secret owner Leslie Wexner, and Michael Bloomberg—he of the multiple nondisclosure agreements—were all on the front page of a leading newspaper, along with a German mass shooter who'd also murdered his mother. Nothing indicated that most of these figures and some of these stories were all about the same thing: gender violence and gendered silence.

Donald Trump bought Stormy Daniels's silence just before the 2016 election; she received some money in return for becoming a person who would never have words, never tell her story (and then, as many women have done since 2017, she finally did, and received death threats for doing so). There's an illuminating overlap to be found in the fact that Alan Dershowitz was friends with and provided legal services for both Jeffrey Epstein and Mr. Trump—the former for sexual abuse, the latter in his first impeachment trial. Historian Heather Cox Richardson wrote of that trial, "But for

Trump and his enablers, this trial is not about the truth; it never has been. It is about dominance and power. Forcing someone to accept what they know to be untrue reinforces the dominance of the person telling the lies."

To be powerless means that your facts and truths can be overwhelmed by the powerful, who prefer these facts or voices or stories not be heard. And what it means in the end is that truth and fact and evidence only prevail in a democracy—a democracy not just in the electoral sense but a world in which power differentials don't corrupt what stories get told and which get suppressed. Where what facts prevail depends on the strength of those facts, not the status of the speaker.

Imagine if Weinstein had committed his first sexual assault in a world in which his victim had the audibility, credibility, value, and resources he did. There would likely not have been a second, or six women testifying in a trial, or ninety women with stories no one made space for before something changed in 2017. More likely, there would not have been a first in a world where he knew he could not overpower her facts and voice, even if he could overpower her physically. When I hear these stories, I think of my own youth as a person who was voiceless, not because I could not speak, but because they would not listen.

For myself, I wanted Weinstein found guilty and imprisoned, not as revenge—though he richly deserves it—but as a warning to men like him that the age of impunity is over, that there are people willing to listen to women, and that sometimes what we say has consequences. The most important change will be found in what we cannot measure—all the crimes that don't happen because would-be perpetrators fear the consequences, now that there are consequences. All the potential victims who know that if they speak up, someone might hear them and heed them. I want more than that, though: I want a society where the desire and entitlement to commit sexual violence wither away, not out of fear but out of respect for the rights and humanity of victims.

But even the idea that Weinstein's conviction is a watershed is optimistic: from restaurant kitchens to agricultural fields to college campuses, sexual violence is still harming millions directly and making survival extra work that too many women must do daily. We have democratized storytelling and truth to the extent that we now sometimes hear about the consequences of inequality, but not enough to end those stories. We—well, some of us—have begun a process that matters more than anything, but we have miles to go.

The Storykiller and His Sentence

There was a man who was in charge of stories. He decided that some stories would be born, expensive, glamorous stories that cost more than what a hundred minimum-wage earners might make in a hundred years, filmy stories with the labor of hundreds of skilled workers expended so that they would slip in like dreams to the minds of millions and make money, and he made money and the money gave him more power over more stories.

There were other stories he decided must die. Those were the stories women might tell about what he had done to them, and he determined that no one must hear them, or if they heard them they must not believe them or if they believed them it must not matter.

His work to let stories out was public, and he was on many stages accepting many awards for them and at many parties exerting influence and handing out favors and malevolent disfavor. His work to keep stories in was also strenuous, expensive, and masterful in a way: perhaps he took particular pleasure in stifling the stories of women who were otherwise so visible, so audible, who were in those stories we all saw, in making them dolls who said the words of others, the words that brought him awards and a fortune, and in preventing them from telling their own stories, the stories of what felonies he had committed.

He sat like a malevolent god, deciding whose voice and vision would live and whose would die, or like a king with courtiers to produce this story in a shower of money and networking and to kill this other story with nondisclosure agreements that also required showers of money, sometimes directly out of his business-partner brother's pocket to keep them off the company records. Or he spent political capital to persecute and discredit the women who had stories of what he had done, and to drive them out of their profession, their vocation, and their living, to push them over a cliff at the bottom of which was isolation and inaudibility.

There were grips and gaffers and best boys, sound engineers and editors and acting coaches to make the stories; there were spies, lawyers, insurance companies, underlings to unmake the other stories, some of them skilled actors themselves, and they even went after the newspapers and journalists who got wind of those stories. The whole society was complicit in allowing a system of silencing to exist. That society had created a formal legal contract called a nondisclosure agreement (NDA), which meant that her (and sometimes his or their but so often her) story would be silent forever. One of his victims was not permitted, in the terms of her contract, to talk even to her family or therapists about what happened. Many of them at last violated their NDAs to speak, and the complicity of celebrity lawyers and the legal strategy for strangling stories, the silence for sale, looked bad when it was dragged out in the light of day, and some states passed laws limiting them, at least as they pertained to sex. "Who controls the past controls the future," wrote George Orwell in *1984*, "who controls the present controls the future." He who has the story has the power; she who has no story, not even her own, has no power.

And so the storykiller clawed his way through the years, destroyer and generator of stories, sitting like a judge over them all, shaping the public imagination, both with what we saw and heard and what we did not. What we do not know is always the heavier side of the scale, and those of us who find ourselves there find ourselves silent, mute, gagged, our stories murdered before they can go out into the world, or our stories stillborn because we did not dare to speak or because we despaired that if we spoke our words would not do the work words should do in the world—connect us, weave us into the society—but would endanger us or make them ostracize us. And so, the scale dipped low with the weight of strangled, murdered, stillborn, stunted stories. The stories sat inside, like impacted wisdom teeth, like ectopic pregnancies, something that needed to come out. But they could not because the women were not in charge of stories.

In the middle of 2017, this powerful man somehow decided (or a minion decided and invoked his name) that I should watch a film or, rather, a screener—an early-release DVD—of one of the stories he had put out into the world. I knew almost nothing about the man, but I began to be pestered to watch the story. Here's how the letter that was supposed to be from him described it: "The gripping story about a young girl's murder on a Native reservation... I think you'll find it intensely chilling. I'd love to hear your thoughts after you've had a chance to screen. All my best, Harvey."

I didn't watch it. I'm sick of the pretense of sympathetic interest in movies and books and the rest that murder women over and over, and too many Native women are being murdered without adding a fictional murder to the spatter pattern. I see women die violently every day. I'm getting weary of it. Sometimes I take a screenshot of the front page of a newspaper and ask people how many headlines have to do with violence against women or men who have abused women, and sometimes it's most of the lead stories. Sometimes this violence is the story, or sometimes someone who has a record of abusing women is just running for president or is president and the story is about something else, but their power reminds you of your powerlessness if you're a woman.

But also directly in the news are gruesome stories—a few weeks ago I ran into news about an American man who dismembered his ex with a saw, an Australian man who poured gasoline over his ex and the kids and burned them to death, and a Mexican man who skinned his ex like a rabbit after murdering her. And right after that there was a day when I opened an envelope a publisher sent me to find a memoir by a woman whose sister had been murdered, which I decided not to read, and then I sat down next to a woman on the ferry reading the book by James Ellroy about his mother being murdered, with a picture of her corpse on the back cover.

I wasn't looking for these stories; they're there all the time because women are getting killed all the time. I'm just the anomaly who's been noting their frequency for the last thirty years or so, and who has felt impacted by that. I am the Ancient Mariner of violence against women, because for thirty-five years I've been trying to fix people with my glittering eye and make them listen.

And then the king of the storykillers was sentenced to twenty-three years in prison, which means, if he serves all his time, he will be ninety when he gets out.* He was handcuffed to a wheelchair, having declined physically, as though his fall from power had been a physical collapse or perhaps to try to spark a story with sympathy for him in it. He bled with sympathy for himself and people like him, "I was the first example," he said, of men whose crimes

---

* Since I wrote this, his New York sentence was overturned on appeal, but he will be retried, and in California he was sentenced to sixteen years after being found guilty of rape. He will likely die in prison.

finally came to light, "and now there are thousands of men who are being accused." That the great majority of them are being accused because they did the things they are accused of is something too terrible to grasp for the old story kings, too damaging to their own story about themselves.

"I'm worried about this country," the *Guardian* reported the storykiller as saying, because there are "thousands of men and women who are losing due process" after being accused. "I'm totally confused. I think men are confused about these issues." That perhaps as many as a hundred women didn't have due process because he was as much a storykiller as a literal assailant and groper and harasser and rapist seemed to be an idea he could not imagine. Because this man who had made so many of our stories, the ones we paid to see, the ones that got the Oscars, could not imagine the stories of these women, could not imagine their stories about him, could not imagine.

"He is baffled at finally being held accountable," one of the victims said. It is not a story he imagined; it is a story he cannot comprehend. But he was no longer in charge of stories. Something changed, and the forces that prevented them from telling their stories were overcome by those who willed those stories into the room and their own fury to speak. And then he became the protagonist of the last story he ever imagined, and his story is now a single interminable sentence, and that twenty-three-year-long sentence is about a storyteller who failed to imagine their stories or the end of his own.

Feminism Has Just Begun

As it happened, I was in Edinburgh on the day *Roe v. Wade* was overturned in the US Supreme Court, and the next day I caught a train back to London and did what I usually do when I get anywhere near King's Cross railway station. I took the short walk to the old St. Pancras churchyard to visit the tombstone of the great feminist ancestor Mary Wollstonecraft, author of that first great feminist manifesto, *A Vindication of the Rights of Women*. To be there that day was to remember that feminism did not start recently—Wollstonecraft died in 1797—and it did not stop on June 24, 2022.

Women in the US gained this (limited) right to abortion access forty-nine years before that day—a short time when the view is from Wollstonecraft's memorial. I have regularly heard the opinions in recent decades that feminism failed or achieved nothing or is over, which seems ignorant of how utterly different the world (or most of it) is now for women than it was that half century ago and more. I say world, because it's important to remember that feminism is a global movement and *Roe v. Wade* and its reversal were only national decisions.

Ireland in 2018, Argentina in 2020, Mexico in 2021, and Colombia in 2022 have all legalized abortion ("Over the past thirty years, more than sixty countries and territories have liberalized their abortion laws," notes the Center for Reproductive Rights, while only four, including the US, have narrowed them). So many things have changed in the last half century for women in so many countries that it would be hard to itemize them all; suffice it to say that the status of women has been radically altered for the better, overall, in this span of time. Feminism is a human rights movement that endeavors to change things that are not just centuries but in many cases millennia old, and that it is far from done and faces setbacks and resistance is neither shocking nor reason to stop.

Wollstonecraft did not even dream of votes for women—most men in the Britain of her time didn't have voting rights either—or of many other rights we consider ordinary, but you don't have to go back to the eighteenth century to encounter radical inequality on the basis of gender. It was everywhere in large and small ways into recent decades—and culturally still persists in the widespread attempts to control and contain women and the prejudices women still encounter about their intellectual competence, sexuality, and equality.

Half a century ago it was legal in the US to fire women because they were pregnant—it happened to senator Elizabeth Warren, then a young schoolteacher. The right to access birth control—for married couples—was only guaranteed by the 1965 *Griswold* decision that this rogue Supreme Court may also be gunning for. The right to birth control for the unmarried was only settled in the Supreme Court in 1972. The US 1974 Equal Credit Opportunity Act rendered illegal the discrimination by which unmarried women had trouble getting credit and loans, while married women routinely required their husbands to cosign for them.

Marriage, in most parts of the world, including North America and Europe, was, until very recently, a relationship in which the husband gained control by law and custom over his wife's body and nearly everything she did, said, and owned. Marital rape was hardly a concept until feminism made it one in the 1970s, and the UK and US only made it illegal in the early 1990s. The seventeenth-century English jurist Matthew Hale argued, "The husband of a woman cannot himself be guilty of an actual rape upon his wife, on account of the matrimonial consent which she has given, and which she cannot retract." That is, a woman having once consented could never thereafter say no, because she had in essence consented to be owned. Incidentally, the Supreme Court decision revoking reproductive rights repeatedly cites Hale (who is also well-known for sentencing two elderly widows to death for witchcraft in 1662).

Wollstonecraft, who had participated in the French Revolution, wrote, "The divine right of husbands, like the divine right of kings, may, it is hoped, in this enlightened age, be contested without danger."* Contested, but hardly overcome, for almost two more centuries. Via coercive control and domestic violence, men still impose their expectation of dominance and punish independence, while right-wing Republicans seek to return women to inferior status under the law and in the culture, citing that ancient text the Bible as their authority.

Their Supreme Court may go after marriage equality next.† I have long thought that the marriage equality that means equal access to same-sex couples would be impossible, had marriage as an institution not been made over, thanks to feminism, as a freely negotiated relationship between equals. Equality between partners is threatening to the inequality inherent in traditional

---

* It's impossible to read this sentence without hearing echoes of it in Ursula K. Le Guin's famous 2014 declaration: "We live in capitalism, its power seems inescapable—but then, so did the divine right of kings. Any human power can be resisted and changed by human beings. Resistance and change often begin in art. Very often in our art, the art of words."

† Since I wrote this, the US right wing has taken aim at in vitro fertilization (IVF), birth control, and no-fault divorce, as well as marriage equality.

patriarchal marriage, which is why—along with homophobia, of course—they're so hostile to it. And, of course, it, too, is new; a very different Supreme Court recognized this right in June 2015, only seven years ago (and Switzerland and Chile only did so in 2021, Greece in 2024).

The last decade has been a rollercoaster of gains and losses, and there is no neat way to add them up. The gains have been profound, but many of them have been subtle. Since about 2012, a new era of feminism opened up conversations—on social media, in traditional media, in politics, and in private—about violence against women and the many forms of inequality and oppression, legal and cultural, obvious and subtle. Recognition of the impact of violence against women expanded profoundly and brought on real results. #MeToo has been much derided as a celebrity circus, but it was only one manifestation of a feminist surge begun five years earlier, and it helped lead to changes in US state and federal laws governing sexual harassment and abuse, including a bill addressing workplace harassment that passed the Senate this February and the president signed into law in early March.*

The February 2023 sentencings of singer R. Kelly to thirty years in prison and sex trafficker Ghislaine Maxwell to twenty are the consequence of a shift in who would be listened to and believed, which is to say who would be valued and whose rights would be defended. Of people being included in the conversations in the courts of law who had not before been heard there. Perpetrators

---

* As *The Hill* reported on March 3, 2022, "President Biden on Thursday signed into a law a bill that will end the use of forced arbitration in lawsuits involving claims of sexual assault and harassment, calling it a 'momentous day for justice and fairness in the workplace.' The law ensures accusers can bring cases alleging sexual assault or harassment in court, rather than being forced into arbitration proceedings that are typically conducted behind closed doors. It voids clauses in employment contracts and other agreements requiring such a process."

who had gotten away with crimes for decades—the serial abuser of young gymnastics competitors Larry Nassar, Bill Cosby, Harvey Weinstein among them—lost their impunity, and belated consequences came crashing down on them. But the fate of a handful of high-profile men is not what matters most, and punishment is not how we remake the world.

The conversations are about violence and inequality, about the intersectionalities of race and gender, about the rethinking of gender beyond the simplest binaries, about what freedom could look like, what desire could be, what equality would mean. Just to have those conversations is liberatory. To see younger women reach beyond what my generation perceived and claimed is exhilarating. These conversations change us in ways the law cannot, make us understand ourselves and each other in new ways, reconceive race, gender, sexuality, and possibility.

You can take away a right through legal means, but you cannot take away the belief in that right so easily. The Supreme Court's *Dred Scott* and *Plessy v. Ferguson* decisions in the nineteenth century did not convince Black people that they did not deserve to live as free and equal citizens; it merely prevented them from doing so in practical terms. Women in many US states have lost their access to abortion, but not their belief in their right to it (and the existence of a drug for safe medication-induced abortions is granting access even to some women in states where abortion is banned). The uproar in response to the court's decision is a reminder of how unpopular it is and how hideously it will impact the ability of women to be free and equal under the law.

It is a huge loss. It does not exactly return us to the world before *Roe v. Wade* because, in both imaginative and practical terms, US society is profoundly different. Women have far more equality under the law, in access to education, employment, and institutions of power, and to political representation. We have far more belief in those rights and a stronger vision of what equality looks like. That the status of women is so radically changed from where it was in, say, 1967, let alone 1797, is evidence that feminism is working. And the Supreme Court's callous decision confirms that there is still a lot of work to do.

Postscript: The two things I've written about most in the past decade are climate and feminism, and, with either one, I believe that the changes we need are not merely practical but imaginative, in that realm where ethics, ideas, and emotions are not separate. We cannot adequately address violence against women through law enforcement and carceral punishment or by advancing the legal and financial status of women. We need to transform society until the desire and entitlement to commit this violence has withered away and become as rare as it is now common, as repellent as it is now excused and eroticized.

III.
More Visions

Deep Time Versus Short Term

The slashing rain turned the dirt roads into muddy creeks, the bus's wipers shoved the torrent back and forth across the windshield, and Don Schreiber handled the wheel like Sandra Bullock in *Speed* as he wisecracked from under a big gray moustache. The vehicle swerved and slid in the storm, lightning flashed on the horizon, thunder shook the air. Whether the old yellow bus would make it back to the ranch house, get stuck, or slide and flip depended on his driving.

Don, in his white Stetson and a blue-and-white checked Western shirt, was our tour guide on this land in northwestern New Mexico that he knew intimately and had dedicated his retirement to protecting. When he and his wife Jane Schreiber bought the ranchland, about two hundred miles northwest of Santa Fe, in 1999 to retire to, they—like many Westerners—found that they owned the land but not the subsurface rights. The fracking boom came, and gas companies began gouging holes for gas wells, laying pipelines and cutting roads across the fragile desert soil. Big trucks rolled across the land night and day to service the wells that studded the landscape. At the well we stopped at, the pressure gauge was broken.

The now seventy-something Don and Jane Schreiber turned what they intended to be a bucolic retirement of riding the range on horseback and practicing small-scale sustainable ranching into environmental advocacy. Jane prefers a quieter approach, but Don is probably the most high-profile opponent of fracking in the San Juan Basin and one of New Mexico's most outspoken climate activists. With outspoken eloquence and humor, his personal experience with fracking's consequences, his lifelong roots in the area, his mastery of the science, geography, and laws behind the fracking boom and the trouble it brings, he's a formidable voice on social media, in public hearings, in interviews, and in editorials.

My New Mexico friends had joined me to come understand firsthand the fossil fuel industry we so often read and talk about. We'd made the long drive out the afternoon before, across beautiful landscapes, with the bare red cliffs and silhouetted mountains Georgia O'Keeffe loved to paint giving way to forests and great expanses of land, like the Schreibers' ranch, that looked flat from a distance but up close revealed billowing swells and gullies descending into small canyons. Studded with rabbit brush, sagebrush, and other tough arid-land plants, the ruddy soil was visible even where a pale covering of dry grass spread. Blue mountains ringed the horizon, and above it all was the immense and turbulent New Mexico summer sky.

San Juan County and the surrounding area are the world's largest known coalbed methane field. One hundred and twenty-two fracking wells are scattered on and around the land to which Don and Jane hold title, and there are more than twenty thousand in the region. Each well presents a threat to the long-term well-being of the land, water, and life this place sustains. Don told me: "It is otherworldly to sit in the center of an arid place like the high desert in New Mexico and watch millions of gallons of water taken from our aquifers or rivers or our lakes pumped down to make a single gas well that contaminates that water forever." Water is as precious as it is scarce here, with annual rainfall and snowmelt of about ten inches a year, some of it in monsoon storms like the ones we drove through.

As Don drove, we could see the erosive power of roads cut straight across dry fragile soil held together by surface crust and underground networks of roots. Fast-moving streams somewhere between the color and consistency of chocolate milk and New Mexico's red chile sauce carried that liquified topsoil into gullies and ruts, carving them deeper as they gushed. The roads deteriorated as we sped across them.

The fracking wells and their infrastructure of pipelines and roads represent one kind of menace while they're pumping and another when the corporations are done pulling out the gas and using up the scarce local water—the menace of abandoned wells and roads that continue to pollute and erode the landscape. The gains are short term, made to be burned up; the losses are long term. The region—whose biggest town's name, Farmington, reflects its agrarian roots—has the highest concentration of methane pollution in the United States, and methane is a far more potent, if shorter-lived, greenhouse gas than carbon dioxide.

We had gotten caught in that rain because I wanted to see the ruins that Don had mentioned, and we had gone a little farther out rather than turning back, despite the ominous sky. At the far end of our journey across the Schreiber ranchlands, we had come to a place where an orange-red sandstone cliff paralleled the rough road. In its heights was a stone structure built many hundreds of years ago by the Diné (Navajo) inhabitants of the area. Flat rocks the same color as the surrounding stone were piled up into neat walls on a ledge partway up the cliff. We got out and admired it until the increasing rain made it urgent to try to race the downpour back to the ranch house.

But memory of that structure stayed with me. It is said that this place, arid as it was, had supported human beings for millennia (archeologists say more than ten thousand years) and could possibly do so for many more. It spoke of deep time. The wells spoke of the opposite, of what we could call shallow time. The fossil fuel industry chases short-term profit and leaves long-term wreckage in its wake, both as the specific damage to extraction sites, which may be gouged out or poisoned or both, and as climate chaos. It's like this all over the world.

For example, in Germany, a private company is mining low-grade lignite coal by digging up a lush rural landscape, mile after mile of it, gouging out the ground where farms, villages, churches, graveyards have existed for centuries. The gain is dirty coal to be burned once. The loss is farmland that has fed human beings for a thousand years and probably could for a thousand more.

What will be left behind is some profit in the accounts of shareholders, some emissions from the dirtiest fuel on Earth, and a vast hole that will fill with water and become a manmade lake. No one standing on the rim of that lake a century or five from now will have benefited from the coal. They might feel the loss of the farmland, the thousand-year-old church, the continuity of the surface of this particularly fertile stretch of the earth, and the impact of the carbon dioxide that was emitted when the coal was burned. They may feel, as the ravages of climate chaos or its residues, the harm from that coal.

By the same measure, no one standing where we did, in fifty or five hundred years, to see those Diné ruins will have benefited from the methane extracted there, but the landscape may be more eroded, more arid, more contaminated, more impoverished because of a brief quest for profit in the early twenty-first century. We have been making short-term decisions for a long time, and the consequences have arrived, along with the decision as to whether it's time to commit to long-term futures and the long-term survival of places that fossil fuel has and will wreck.

The truth about fossil fuel is that the transition away from it is already underway. Already underway and already profitable—solar and wind are cheaper than fossil fuel for power generation in most places—and beneficial for us all. Electrifying almost everything and getting that electricity from renewable sources isn't just something we need to do for the climate, for the composition of the upper atmosphere and the way that atmosphere shapes our weather, ocean currents, and destiny. It's something we need to do to escape the many kinds of devastation that came with the age of fossil fuel. That includes not only the damage to water, earth, and air but also to our politics, as reliance on the unevenly distributed resource props up tyrannical regimes, tolerated for access to fuel, and bullying corporations that spread propaganda and corrupt politics. Fossil fuel is now the worst way to power machines, in the many cases when those machines can run on electricity from renewables.

That hot summer day in northwestern New Mexico, we did make it back, thanks to Don's quick reflexes and decades of experience navigating treacherous dirt roads. It wasn't a certainty we would until we were heading up the last rise and the stable and ranch house were in view through the raindrops.

But, in a sense, we are all in a school bus on a slippery road in a thunderstorm. Climate activists are trying to take the wheel from the reckless drivers who are steering us all into trouble. We are trying to turn toward safety. We are trying to be good ancestors, to make a world in which the land that, in the past, fed many species, including ours, will feed them in the future, to take the fork in the road ahead that leads to well-being in the short term and the long. To build better roads to the future instead of sliding into the ditch.

Changing the Climate Story

Every crisis is in part a storytelling crisis. This is as true of climate chaos as anything else. We are hemmed in by stories that prevent us from seeing, or believing in, or acting on the possibilities for change. Some are habits of mind, some are industry propaganda. Sometimes, the situation has changed but the stories haven't, and people follow the old versions, like outdated maps, into dead ends.

We need to leave the age of fossil fuel behind, swiftly and decisively. But what drives our machines won't change until we change what drives our ideas. The visionary organizer adrienne maree brown wrote not long ago that there is an element of science fiction in climate action: "We are shaping the future we long for and have not yet experienced. I believe that we are in an imagination battle."

In order to do what the climate crisis demands of us, we have to find stories of a livable future, stories of popular power, stories that motivate people to do what it takes to make the world we need. Perhaps we also need to become better critics and listeners, more careful about what we take in and who's telling it, what we believe and repeat, because stories can give power—or they can take it away. To change our relationship to the physical world—to end an era of profligate consumption by the few that has consequences for the many—means changing how we think about pretty much everything: wealth, power, joy, time, space, nature, value, what constitutes a good life, what matters, how change itself happens.

As the climate journalist Mary Heglar writes, we are not short on innovation. "We've got loads of ideas for solar panels and microgrids. While we have all of these pieces, we don't have a picture of how they come together to build a new world. For too long, the climate fight has been limited to scientists and policy experts. While we need their skills, we also need so much more. When I survey the field, it's clear that what we desperately need is more artists."

What the climate crisis is, what we can do about it, and what kind of a world we can have are all about what stories we tell and whose stories are heard. Climate change was a story that fell on mostly indifferent ears when it was first discussed in the mainstream more than thirty years ago. Even a dozen years ago, it was supposed to be happening very slowly and in the distant future. There were a lot of references to "our grandchildren's time." It was a problem that was difficult to grasp—this dispersed, incremental, atmospheric, invisible, global problem with many causes and manifestations, the solutions to which are also dispersed and manifold. That voices from the climate movement have finally succeeded in making the vast majority understand it, and many to care passionately about it, might be the biggest single victory the movement will have. Because once you've won the popular imagination, you've changed the game and its possible outcomes. But this was a long, slow, arduous process, and misconceptions still abound.

A lot of people don't know that we've largely won the battle to make people aware and concerned. The *Los Angeles Times* ran a well-intentioned editorial last year about how most Americans don't care about climate breakdown. That was true once, but it no longer is. A Pew Research poll in 2020 concluded that two-thirds of Americans wanted to see more government action on climate, but last summer the scientific journal *Nature* published a study concluding that most Americans *believe* that only a minority (37 to 43 percent) supports climate action, when in reality a large majority (66 to 80 percent) does. That gap between perceived and actual support undermines motivation and confidence. We need better stories—and sometimes better means more up to date.

Outright climate denial—the old story that climate change isn't real—has largely been rendered obsolete (outside of social media) by climate-driven catastrophes around the globe and good work by climate activists and journalists. But other stories still stop us from seeing clearly. Greenwashing—the schemes created by fossil fuel corporations and others to portray themselves as on the environment's side while they continue their profitable destruction—is rampant. It's harder to recognize a false friend than an honest enemy, and their false solutions, delaying tactics, and empty promises can be confusing for nonexperts. Fortunately, as the climate movement has diversified, one new organization, Clean Creatives, focuses specifically on pressuring advertising and PR agencies to stop doing the industry's dirty work. Likewise, climate journalists are exposing how fossil fuel money is funding pseudo-environmental opposition to offshore wind turbines and solar installations. (As climate activist and oil policy analyst Antonia Juhasz recently told me, the climate movement is now going after every aspect of the fossil fuel industry, including funding by banks and, via the divestment movement, shares held by investors; donations to politicians; insurers; permits for extraction; transport; refinement; emissions, notably through lawsuits concerning their impact; shutting coal-fired power plants; and pushing for a rapid transition to electrification.)

But we still lack stories that give context. For example, I see people excoriate the mining, principally for lithium and cobalt, that are used in the batteries to store renewable energy and in electric cars, apparently oblivious to the much vaster scale and impact of fossil fuel mining. If you're concerned about mining on indigenous land, about local impacts or labor conditions, I give you the biggest mining operations ever undertaken: for oil, gas, and coal, and the hungry machines that must constantly consume them to run (while these materials for renewables are durable and largely recyclable; the energy itself comes not from them but from wind and sun). Extracting material that will be burned up creates the incessant cycle of consumption on which the fossil fuel industry has grown fabulously rich. It creates climate chaos as well as destruction and contamination at every stage of the process. Globally, burning fossil fuels kills more than eight million people annually, a death toll larger than any recent war. But that death toll is largely invisible for lack of compelling stories about it.

All mining needs to be done with respect for the land and people in the vicinity, but the impact of mining for renewables needs to be weighed against the far more devastating impact of mining for and burning fossil fuel. The race is on to find battery materials that are less impactful than the current ones, and some of the results look promising. There are batteries—for example, those in about half of Tesla car models as of 2022—that don't use cobalt anymore. Many other battery materials are being researched and developed, and in some cases deployed, as are some more innovative means—salt caverns that can store energy long term, and water systems in which abundant sun and wind pump water uphill, which generates hydropower when it flows downhill.

Other stories of premature defeat are all too common. In the 400,000-strong 2014 climate march in New York City, one section marched behind a huge banner declaring "WE HAVE THE SOLUTIONS"—but many people still believe we do not. We have the solutions we need in solar and wind; we just need to build them out and make the transition, fast. Looking to wildly ineffectual carbon sequestration and other undeveloped and yet-to-be-realized technologies as relevant solutions is like ignoring the lifeboats at hand in the hope that fancy new ones are coming when the ship is sinking and speed is of the essence.

One story I frequently encounter frames the possibilities in absolutes: if we can't win everything, then we lose everything. There are so many doom-soaked stories out there—about how civilization, humanity, even life itself, are scheduled to die out. This apocalyptic thinking is due to another narrative failure: the inability to imagine a world different than the one we currently inhabit.

People without much sense of history imagine the world as static. They assume that if the present order is failing, the system is collapsing and there is no alternative. A historical imagination equips you to understand that change is ceaseless. You only have to look to the past to see such a world, dramatically different half a century ago, stunningly so a century ago. The UK, for example, ran almost entirely on coal power until the 1960s, and if you had said then that it would have to quit coal, many would have imagined this meant an utter collapse of the energy system, not its transformation. Even in 2008, the organization Carbon Brief noted, "Four-fifths of the UK's electricity came from fossil fuels. . . . Since then, the UK has cleaned up its electricity mix faster than any other major world economy. Coal-fired power has virtually disappeared and even gas use is down by a quarter. Instead, the country now gets more than half of its electricity from low-carbon sources, such as solar, wind and nuclear."* Scotland already generates nearly all the electricity it needs from renewables (of course

---

* On September 30, 2024, the last coal-fired electrical plant in the UK closed. The age of coal has ended in the country where it began.

as systems formerly powered by fossil fuel go electric, renewables need to expand).

While I often hear people casually assert that our world is doomed, no reputable scientist makes such claims. Most are deeply worried but far from hopeless. There are already profound losses, but our action or inaction determine how much more loss will occur, and whose it will be, and some repair is possible. Efforts sufficient to reduce the amount of carbon dioxide in the atmosphere could lower temperatures and reverse some aspects of climate breakdown.

Even the journalist David Wallace-Wells, who rose to fame with a deeply pessimistic book about climate a few years ago, has shifted his view. He currently describes a future somewhere between the best- and worst-case scenarios, a future "with the most terrifying predictions made improbable by decarbonization and the most hopeful ones practically foreclosed by tragic delay. The window of possible climate futures is narrowing, and as a result, we are getting a clearer sense of what's to come: a new world, full of disruption ... yet mercifully short of true climate apocalypse."

A climate story we urgently need is one that exposes who is actually responsible for climate chaos. It's been popular to say that we are all responsible, but Oxfam reports that over the past twenty-five years, the carbon impact of the top 1 percent of the wealthiest human beings was twice that of the bottom 50 percent, so responsibility for the impact and the capacity to make change is currently distributed very unevenly.

By saying, "We are all responsible," we avoid the fact that the global majority of us don't need to change much, but a minority needs to change a lot. This is also a reminder that the idea that we need to renounce our luxuries and live more simply doesn't really apply to the majority of human beings outside what we could perhaps call the overdeveloped world. What is true of Beverly Hills is not true of the majority from Bangladesh to Bolivia.

When it comes to who's harming the climate, it's also been popular to focus on individual contributions. The fossil fuel industry likes the narrative of personal responsibility as a way to keep us scrutinizing ourselves and one another, rather than them. They've promoted the concept of climate footprints as a way to keep the focus on us and not them, and it's worked. Usually, if I ask people what they're doing about the climate emergency, most will talk about what they're not consuming or doing—but these will never add up to the speed and scale of change needed to change the system.

One of the goals of system change is to supersede individual virtue. Just as you no longer have to opt in to buying a car with seatbelts or ask for the no-smoking section on the train or restaurant, at some point in the near future you won't have to opt in to traveling in an electric car or bus, or living or working in all-electric buildings. Electrification will have happened because of the collective action that takes shape as policy and regulation.

The veteran climate activist Bill McKibben recently wrote a brilliant analysis pointing out that if you have money in one of the banks funding fossil fuels—especially, in the US, Wells Fargo, Chase, Citi, and Bank of America—your retirement funds or savings account may have a much larger climate footprint than you do. The impact of your diet and how you get to work may pale in comparison to the impact of your money in the bank. The vegan on the bicycle may still be contributing to climate chaos if her life savings are in a bank lending her money to the fossil fuel industry.

Individual impact, leaving the ultrawealthy aside, matters mostly in the aggregate. And in aggregate we can change that. Our greatest power lies in our roles as citizens, not consumers, when we can band together to collectively change how our world works. Various campaigns around the world have focused on fossil finance, with significant successes behind them, and much more to achieve ahead. The climate movement has become far more sophisticated and precise in its targets in recent years. It's doing a brilliant job; it just needs enough people and resources behind it to be more powerful than the status quo.

Not long ago, I took three activists who were formerly part of the Sunrise Movement, a youth group campaigning to address climate breakdown, to see the 1991 film *Terminator 2* at a cinema. The film was as great as I remembered, not least because the lead character, Linda Hamilton playing a ferocious mother to her messianic son, chooses as her motto "No fate but what we make." In that movie, the future has come back to meddle with the present through the sci-fi technologies of time travel and robot-warrior terminators. We see how actions in the present shape the future through tremendous battles over what that future will be. This is, of course, just as true in real life. We don't get terminators and other time travelers to tell us what the consequences of our actions are, but they still have consequences. You ban the insecticide DDT, and a lot of bird species stop dying out. You ban chlorofluorocarbons, and the hole in the ozone layer stops growing.

In another way, *Terminator 2* is less useful as a lens for thinking about the climate crisis. It's part of the conventions of storytelling in film—and comics, fiction, graphic novels, and too many news narratives—that tells us that the world can only be saved by exceptional individuals, often loners, whose gifts are often the capacity to inflict and endure extreme violence. Linda Hamilton and costar Arnold Schwarzenegger shoot, clobber, crush, outrun, and outfight everything thrown at them, and that's their celebrated skill set, along with a bit of dry humor.

Humor aside, this has little to do with how the world really gets changed most of the time. The skills of real-world superheroes are solidarity, strategy, patience, persistence, vision, and the ability to inspire hope in others. The rescuers we need are mostly not individuals, they are collectives—movements, coalitions, campaigns, civil society. Within those groups there may be someone with an exceptional gift for motivating others, but even the world's greatest conductor needs an orchestra. One person cannot do much; a movement can topple a regime. We are sadly lacking stories in which collective actions or the patient determination of organizers is what changes the world.

Another thing we get from our films and fictions is the expectation of a single solution and a clear resolution to our problems: a sudden victory, a celebration, and the trouble is over. The climate crisis does not fit easily into this format. Ceasing to extract and burn fossil fuel is central, but there is no single solution. Protecting carbon-sequestering peat bogs, forests, and grasslands also matters; so does transforming high-impact materials such as cement; implementing better design for buildings, transport, and cities; and addressing soil conservation, farming, and food production and consumption. There are milestones and important goals, but the familiar Hollywood ending—crossing the finish line to wrap up the story—doesn't describe this reality.

Change often functions more like a relay race, with new protagonists picking up where the last left off. In 2019, a Berkeley city councilwoman decided to propose banning fossil-gas connections in new construction, and the proposal was passed by the council unanimously. This small city's commitment to all-electric new buildings could seem insignificant—and it was overturned by the courts—but more than fifty other California municipalities picked it up, as did the city of New York. The state of New York failed to pass a similar measure, but Washington state succeeded, and the idea that new construction should not include gas has spread internationally. Internationally, recognition has spread that this stuff we pump into homes is methane—"natural gas" is just a euphemism—and it's harmful to human health as well as explosive as well as a far more immediately impactful greenhouse gas than carbon dioxide.

Such relay races have long been how human rights campaigns work: a good protest, campaign, or even piece of legislation can introduce new ideas that do their own work in the world at large. Even failed campaigns may succeed in opening the path for later change. The Green New Deal did not pass in the US Senate, but it became a template for the Biden administration's climate legislation and shifted the conversation about what is possible. It led the way to the Inflation Reduction Act, the biggest climate bill the US has ever passed. Opponents have often portrayed protecting the environment as a job killer; the Green New Deal did a lot to change that story by portraying climate action as a job creator.

Recognizing the reality of climate breakdown means recognizing the interconnectedness of all things. That connection brings obligation: to respect nature, to build domestic regulation and international treaties that protect what's needed, to negotiate the freedom of the individual in the name of the well-being of the collective. This is, of course, a worldview in direct contrast with free-market fundamentalism and libertarianism. Even the facts of climate science are ideologically offensive to people committed to individual freedom without accountability, let alone the demands created by treaties and regulations. Responsibility and obligation are dismal words in mainstream culture, so perhaps there will be other stories that recognize this process as reciprocity and relationship, in which we give back, in gratitude and respect for all the

Earth does for us. Even short of that, we can recognize our self-interest in maintaining the system on which life depends.

If news is the daily report on what's just happened, we need a way of pulling back from individual events to see the broad context of how it happened. We need benchmarks or memories of how things used to be even to see change of any kind, including climate change. A strong sense of the past allows for a strong sense of the future, that remembering difficulty and transformation equips us to face them again.

One of the things that buoys me is the long arc of change in renewable technology. Mostly what you see in the news about renewables is short term: stories on the latest drop in price, or proliferation of solar and wind over the past year or two. If you enlarge your time frame, you see that those annual changes have amounted to an astonishing plummet in prices and rise in efficiency and global use, compounded by innovations in materials and storage. Over the past fifteen years, solar has been installed at approximately three times the rate predicted, and its price has plummetted as dramatically as its implementation has risen.

Twenty years ago, we did not have constructive ways to leave the age of fossil fuel behind. Now we do. And the solutions keep getting better. In 2021, the organization Carbon Tracker put out a report that showed current technology could produce one hundred times as much electricity from solar and wind than current global demand. The report concludes: "The technical and economic barriers have been crossed and the only impediment to change is political." At the end of the last millennium, those barriers seemed insurmountable. The change is revolutionary, but the revolution was too slow to be visible to most. The report continues: "At the current 15–20% growth rates of solar and wind, fossil fuels will be pushed out of the electricity sector by the mid-2030s and out of total energy supply by 2050. . . . The unlocking of energy reserves 100 times our current demand creates new possibilities for cheaper energy and more local jobs in a more equitable world, with far less environmental stress."

We tend to think utopias are unbelievable, but this is a sober-minded think tank focused on climate and energy politics. The report made little impact on the general public. Because the energy revolution has been incremental, there's been no single breakthrough moment. Yet, on the one hand, it adds up to an encouraging and even astonishing narrative. On the other hand, people find grim narratives all too believable, whether or not they are grounded in fact. We are still inundated by harmful, as well as untrue, stories about climate and the future. Prophecies can be self-fulfilling: if you insist that we cannot possibly win, you pit yourself against the possibility of victory and the people trying to achieve it.

Early on, we heard that renewables were very expensive—this was part of the austerity narrative, or an excuse for not making the transition. But improvements in design and economies of scale are among the factors making them the cheapest form of electricity almost everywhere on Earth. There's no reason to think the innovations of design and economic improvements are all behind us; I suspect they're mostly ahead of us. Engineer and energy expert Saul Griffith recently wrote: "Most people believe a clean-energy future will require everyone to make do with less, but it actually means we can have better things." The old story was that we couldn't afford to do what the climate emergency required. The new one is that it would not only be ecologically devastating, but more expensive not to. Texas and Iowa get a huge amount of their electricity from wind because it makes economic sense, not because these red states are passionate about addressing the climate crisis. Over their lifetime, electric cars work out to be cheaper than internal combustion cars because charging and maintaining them is cheaper. And, of course, these two examples don't include the indirect effects of burning fossil fuels on human health and the climate.

A lot of people tend to measure climate action in terms of huge national or international news events, but the change that matters is often happening at local and regional and other levels. A university divests; a state sets a date for ending the sale of new gasoline-burning cars; a city passes a measure mandating all-electric new buildings; ground is broken on a major solar installation; a state or country sets a new record for percentage of wind power in its energy mix; a pipeline or gas terminal or drilling site gets cancelled; a carbon-sequestering forest or peat bog gets protected status; a coal plant closes.

This does not erase all the bad news about the continuing breakdown of natural systems and its toll on human lives and impact on a livable future, but it does contextualize them as crises we can respond to if we choose to. So much is happening, both wonderful and terrible, and it adds up to more stories than almost anyone can take in. But the overarching frameworks in which we receive them matter, and so do the critical skills to recognize, choose, and change stories.

The climate crisis is a problem with no single solution but many, just as there is no one savior but many protagonists in the struggle. In 2019, Swedish climate activist Greta Thunberg said we must embrace "cathedral thinking," adding: "We must lay the foundation while we may not know exactly how to build the ceiling." The speculative fiction writer Octavia Butler included this passage in one of her essays:

> "OK," the young man challenged. "So what's the answer?"
> "There isn't one," I told him.

"No answer? You mean we're just doomed?" He smiled as though he thought this might be a joke.

"No," I said. "I mean there's no single answer that will solve all of our future problems. There's no magic bullet. Instead there are thousands of answers—at least. You can be one of them if you choose to be."

Climate of Abundance

Every once in a while, I catch a glimpse of what it would be like if things were really different. Different as in better. I wander in a country where violence seems so unlikely I realize how much it is a constant background presence in public life and my psyche in the US. I spend time with friends in countries where access to housing, education, and health care underwrites their idealistic choices and confidence. I visit places where rivers run free and wildlife thrives, or where food is produced in ways that respect the workers and the land.

Or I talk to people who found in a disaster that they themselves and the community around them could be more connected, more generous, more heroic than they ever imagined. "The ultimate, hidden truth of the world is that it is something that we make, and could just as easily make differently," the anthropologist David Graeber famously said, and the climate crisis is an invitation to make almost everything differently. An invitation and a demand.

Some of the reluctance to do what the climate crisis requires of us comes from the assumption that it mostly means giving things up. But what if it means giving up things we're well rid of, from deadly emissions to nagging feelings of doom and complicity in destruction? A monastic once told me renunciation can mean giving up things that make you miserable.

Of course, in the face of the climate crisis, sticking with the status quo isn't an option. We either make the changes science has shown are necessary and engineering has made possible, or we let runaway change of the worst kind devastate people and places. We've already seen so much of that, from firestorms in California to floods in Pakistan to famines in Africa. So, the idea that what we currently have is abundance and what's required is austerity can be stood on its head; this age is miserable for so many in so many ways, and doing what the crisis requires could make many and even most lives better.

To invert the assumptions means rethinking what constitutes wealth and poverty, well-being and its opposite. By other measures than goods and money, we are now impoverished. *We* is itself a tricky word, since, of course, the affluent minority of people on Earth now have an obscene excess of stuff, while the lives of the majority range from modest to desperate. But even the affluent live in a world where confidence in the future and in the society and institutions around us, a sense of security, social connectedness, mental and physical health, and other measures of well-being are often dismal.

Burning fossil fuel makes us poorer in many ways. As it fills the upper atmosphere with carbon dioxide that destabilizes temperature and weather, it drives a crisis of despair, grief, and anxiety among the young facing an uncertain future. Worldwide, breathing air contaminated by burning fossil fuels kills more than eight million people a year and damages the health of many more, particularly babies and children. Wherever fossil fuel is extracted and refined becomes a de facto sacrifice zone, from the Alberta tar sands to the contaminated rainforests of Ecuador, from the refineries of Louisiana to the West Virginia mountaintops scraped off for coal to the contaminated Niger delta.

Across the earth, the fossil fuel industry also poisons our politics. The huge profit—about $3 billion a day worldwide—the industry takes in is spent in part on buying politicians. The industry has long shown a preference for authoritarians and anti-environmentalists. In the US, more than two-thirds of political donations since 1990 have gone to Republicans, who often do a better job of representing oil, gas, and coal than their human constituents. Though coal baron and Democratic senator Joe Manchin was much berated for his lack of support for climate legislation, his vote mattered so much because not a single Republican senator supported the measures to address the climate crisis.

In the present order of things, most of us suffer from moral injury—the impact on the psyche of witnessing or feeling complicit in something wrong. Or we avoid seeing and thinking about it and take on the moral numbing and willful obliviousness that is the avoidant form of moral injury. A deep sense of wrongness permeates our lives. We know that, from our fossil fuel to our smartphones to much of our food, exploitative working conditions and environmental harm are part of their production. We see the US's increasing economic inequality, the desperate misery of those who lack housing or are crushed by debt, see the despair that fuels addiction, know that child hunger is a major issue. And we know the planet is in trouble, and that has particularly impacted the young with justified fury, grief, and despair in recent years.

The climate crisis requires some very specific things of us, a swift transition away from extracting and burning fossil fuel and toward renewables, improved designs for the built environment and transit, better care for the natural world in all the ways we interact with it. For all these things to seem meaningful rather than arbitrary requires understanding that we are parts of grand, intricately orchestrated natural systems that are both beautiful and irreplaceable. This knowledge that we are not separate from nature but dependent on it is already far more present than it was a few decades ago. From the shift to renewables to the shifts in consciousness, what we need is already underway, but we need to cultivate and amplify it until it's how the world works and how we understand the world.

To do what the climate requires of us does mean giving up some of the profligacy of this era, some of its wasteful excess. It's also an opportunity to rethink who we are and what we need and desire. What if we imagined wealth as consisting of joy, beauty, friendship, community, closeness to flourishing nature, to clean air and water, to good food produced without abuse of labor or nature? And security, in our own environments and societies, along with confidence in a viable future?

Materially, the transition could mean embracing not austerity or sacrifice but modesty in consumption. Consuming less stuff means less money spent, means less time earning, means more time for everything else—and maybe more of almost everything good that money can't buy. Being harried and pressured, scrambling and forever in a rush, juggling more things than you can juggle: these have become normal features of too many working people's lives, but, as Graeber reminds us, it could all be different.

"Getting and spending we lay waste our powers," said William Wordsworth a couple of centuries ago. What would it mean to recover those powers, to be rich in time instead of stuff? We talk about spending time like we talk about spending money, and we could spend it on connecting with and caring for the people and places we love, on creative pursuits, on whatever we find most rewarding, on being better citizens and members of our community, on exploring and learning, on taking care of ourselves, on building stronger, deeper selves and societies, on joy, wonder, love, adventure. For so many of us, being so busy with work has leached away our capacity for all these things.

What most struck me when I researched how people respond to disasters wasn't that most people were brave, altruistic, and able to improvise rescues, new social networks, and the other stuff of survival. It's that people found something they craved so much that even amid death, ruin, and disorder, their joy shined out. They found a sense of meaning, of purpose, deep connection, a sense of being vividly alive in the face of deep uncertainty. They witnessed or embodied the opposite of moral injury: moral beauty, when people act with courage, generosity, principle. They knew in those crises what mattered most. It's easy to forget, and immensely powerful forces in our societies convince us we want tawdry stuff that we get by giving those interests more power and money.

What I also learned is that a disaster is a time when the old order breaks down. The people who benefit most from the status quo scramble furiously to restore it. But the people who did not benefit are often exhilarated to see that society, as Graeber reminded us, could be something else, more inclusive, more egalitarian, more open to connection. The climate crisis is a disaster on a more immense scale than anything our species has faced. It is, first of all, a physical crisis, in which our changes to the upper atmosphere affect temperature and weather, with horrific impacts already evident.

But it is not only physical: it is also a moral crisis, in which what made one part of the world hyperprosperous and hyperproductive turned out to be destructive. Other parts of the world bear the brunt of that destruction, because climate change is unfair. The fossil fuel industry and its minions are focused most of all on amplifying the disaster by keeping the fuel burning and the money flowing to its producers. But, for the rest of us, the crisis is also an opportunity. We could be something else.

There are no guarantees about what will happen, and "what will happen" is the language of inevitability, while the future is shaped by what we do in the present, on what we make happen. There are no guarantees but there are possibilities, if we envision them, believe they're possible, and work to make them more possible and then actual. So much transformation is already underway, in the most practical and most conceptual ways.

Everywhere around me I see people rethinking what agriculture, energy, education, community, urban design, transportation can be, and turning those ideas into realities. We can make a better world, and the project is underway but also under attack; it needs participation, defense, and expansion. And it needs belief. We can have clean air and water. We can feed the world with processes that don't destroy oceans and soils, don't devastate rural places and the people there. We can harness the sun and the wind and have cheap, abundant energy almost everywhere. We can make a world more abundant than the world of 2023. But all these tangible changes are only possible with intangible changes in our sense of what *we* means, what we care about most, who we think we can be, what we believe is possible.

The Great Transformation

When news of Thich Nhat Hanh's death spread around the world, I saw far more people than I'd have expected say how he affected them, through a talk, a book, a retreat, an idea, an example. It was a reminder of the huge impact Buddhism has had in the West as a set of ideas that have spread far beyond the limits of who belongs to a Buddhist group or has a formal practice. You could think of Buddhism in this context as one tributary of a broad new river of ideas flowing through the West, from which many have drunk without knowing quite where the waters came from.

A high-profile critic of the US war on Vietnam and a Vietnamese monk who founded meditation centers on four continents and published dozens of books, Thich Nhat Hanh was one of the great spiritual teachers who came from Asia in the twentieth century, along with Zen monks from Japan and Tibetan rinpoches. His death on January 22, 2022, seemed to me not an ending but a reminder that something far grander than this great teacher began sometime in the last century and continues to spread. Westerners were receptive to Buddhist teachings because they yearned for something that hadn't been a significant part of their own culture.

We are not who we were very long ago. A lot of new ideas have emerged from Buddhism and other traditions emphasizing kindness and compassion, equality and egalitarianism, nonviolence, critical perspectives on materialism and capitalism, and what I once heard the Zen priest Paul Haller at San Francisco Zen Center call "the practice of awareness." They constitute a shift in what we ask of ourselves and others as profound as it is subtle. That subtlety consists of its incrementalness and of its realization as personal beliefs and actions in everyday life that sometimes add up to more concrete changes in laws and institutions.

To recognize how much has changed, you have to go back to how widely accepted various forms of domination and inequality were half a century ago, from corporal punishment in public schools to domestic violence and systemic silencing and exclusion. A lot of us have had the experience, in recent years, of going back to old novels and films and even songs to find that we no longer overlook or accept the casual cruelty and discrimination that seemed so normal at the time. Of course, the new ideas are corruptible, and charismatic leaders, including in Buddhist lineages, have abused their power (but I was amused to find that corporate attempts to co-opt mindfulness sometimes backfire when they make employees less tolerant of institutional amorality).

This river of new ideas is a confluence of many other tributaries, of feminism, antiracism, and ecological ideas, and it has as one of its key principles a vision that everything is connected. Of course, not everything has changed; BIPOC people in the US are far from achieving equality by most measures; and many of these ideas exist more as aspirations than everyday practices, or they flourish in some communities but are under attack or have not yet arrived in others. But none of this means the ideas and ideals don't matter, and the backlash by the right is a backlash against something they see as threateningly transformative.

I've called contemporary conservative thinking "the ideology of isolation," obsessed with control through separation and segregation, through borders and anti-immigration rhetoric, through policing racial and gender categories, and through marriage inequality as both a denial of marital rights to same-sex couples and an affirmation of male domination within heterosexual marriage. It's anti-environmental, because of its opposition to the foundational truth science has revealed more and more boldly in recent decades is that the world is made of pervasive, interconnecting systems, not discrete objects. With that truth comes a mandate to act with responsibility toward the consequences that is at odds with the conservative ideals of individual freedom and unfettered capitalism.

The ideas are good; do they have consequences? I'd argue that they do. On January 25, 2022, the Save the Redwoods League announced that it had transferred title to a 523-acre stretch of redwood forest to the Intertribal Sinkyone Wilderness Council, a coalition of ten tribal groups on the northwest coast of California. The place that had been dubbed Andersonia West "will again be known as Tc'ih-Léh-Dûñ (pronounced tsih-ih-LEY-duhn), meaning 'Fish Run Place' in the Sinkyone language," the press release notes. Changing statues and names in our time—replacing the names of slave-owners and colonists with heroes of liberation, including nonwhite and nonmale figures—is also a sign of this grand shift.

You have to know that the Save the Redwoods League was founded 104 years ago by wealthy white men who were eugenicist elitists to understand how vast a transformation has taken place. Most of that transformation has been in the past few decades. I remember reading an obscure academic paper on the scurrilous past of the Save the Redwoods League in the mid-1990s. At the time, the environmental movement tended to ignore or oppose contemporary indigenous presence on or rights to the lands they sought to conserve and was complacent or oblivious about its own past.

Those struggles are far from over, but the premises with which many of us operate are far different than they were. These usually begin as changes in consciousness and new narratives. They end as changes in law, policy, everyday practices, and stuff as tangible as land ownership. This year, that includes an old-growth forest under indigenous management, with trees more than eight feet in diameter that "tower among Douglas fir, tanoaks, and Pacific madrones over a vibrant understory of huckleberry, manzanita, and ceanothus."

Hope on Far Horizons

> "There are two places that Kevin Strickland—a 62-year-old Black man convicted by an all-white jury in 1979 and sentenced to life in prison without the chance of parole for 50 years—hopes to see: the ocean, which he has never visited in person, and his mother's grave."
>
> —*Washington Post*, **November 23, 2021, on the exoneration and release of Kevin Strickland**

We tell each other stories the way people plant seeds, not sure what will germinate or feed or go to waste, not sure what will be heard or who is listening and what they'll take from what is offered. I say that like a general principle, but people tell me things, or I read them, and some of them are gifts, a candle to light a corner of the room or a flash of lightning or some warmth of sunlight. Some of them are seeds that grow, slowly, in the dark, surfacing later.

You mix your metaphors, and a seed becomes a lantern glowing, or a flashlight, or a firefly hatching. It becomes the tiny phosphorescent organisms that light up the night ocean. You say a thing that takes you someplace and then the next place, and I hope the thought of the ocean was of some value to this man while he was imprisoned, that it took him someplace or shed some light. Somehow, somewhere he gained a compelling awareness of the sea, from a film, a book, a conversation, an image, a song, or all those things compounding, and it awoke a yearning.

While yearnings are generally considered to be afflictions, they can sometimes be compass needles pointing somewhere, providing direction. They can orient, and to be oriented is to have some coherence, and maybe also to yearn is to hope, if only for the satisfaction of that yearning, and to make your world bigger in some way, even if it's big with what you do not have. He must have said to himself that he would never see the ocean with that life sentence. What does it mean to yearn for the boundlessness of the ocean while doing life in a prison cell in the center of a continent?

Surely it means pain and a sense of being landlocked as well as locked up. I used to row by the prisoners at San Quentin in a yard facing San Francisco Bay surrounded with high cyclone fencing and barbed wire, and wonder if the water gave them some comfort. Mostly they were focused on the basketball games going on, but perhaps proximity to wide-open space offers something even if it's not noted consciously. I do know my friend Jarvis Masters there took pleasure in the seabirds, so much so that his memoir is titled *That Bird Has My Wings*. That's what he once told a fellow prisoner in the yard with him about a seagull, to stop the man from throwing stones at it.

My friends Patrick and Gent call the Pacific Ocean the Great Mother when they come visit and we look at the sun going down over the Pacific horizon together. I've lately had this sense of her, I might now say, as this great swelling, rolling, pulsing body, this gargantuan power, this place of origin for all life, this generative mystery, this opaque water in which so much is living just out of sight, this churning force that throws up stones, sand dollars and other shells, seaweed, the occasional corpse of a whale or a sea lion, since dying is part of living. Of her as a body of water in that realm where living and elemental forces don't need to be separate categories, maybe of her as the primordial force in which nothing need be a separate category.

A friend recently told me about the Hindu goddess whose name translates as She Who Is Never Not Broken. When I mention this to someone in Bangalore who is well acquainted with that goddess, she responds with, "The whole is finite; in our brokenness we are infinite." I think she means that being perfect, being whole, means being sealed and shut off in some way, being that version of complete that needs and welcomes no more. To be broken is to reach out, to be open, to be incomplete and therefore to welcome outside in. Maybe a break opens up room for yearnings as reaching beyond. I can't speak for this man who wants to see the Great Mother living and churning and the grave of his own mother, but I think of the way the ocean sings with every wave of her majestic power, of the surface of the Earth that is seven-tenths water, so that we dwell on a planet that could be called Ocean rather than Earth.

The ocean itself breaks and another friend tells me, "In surfing we say the waves break. You ride it as it breaks. You pray for it to break." "Waves begin to break when the ratio of wave height/wavelength exceeds 1/7," says a surfing magazine. That is, they topple from their heights, little rebel angels endlessly falling toward the shore.

Sometimes all the scraps of information that come by seem to cohere into a picture; sometimes a pattern emerges. I yearn for patterns and meanings, since for me a sense of meaninglessness brings on depression. Orientation and purpose and pattern ward it off. A day or two after I read about Mr. Strickland, I read that a ferry from Staten Island to Manhattan will be christened *Dorothy Day*, and so that mystic, social activist, and saint who resided on both of those islands will become a vessel carrying people across the sea. Everyone on the boat will enter into her and then be born from her when she docks on the farther shore. She will be, the news story says, "safer in extreme weather than current ferries."

Day once wrote, "No human creature could receive or contain so vast a flood of love and joy as I often felt after the birth of my child," and the word *flood* seems telling here. The Virgin Mary, who meant so much to the Catholic Day, was called "the chosen vessel," as if she was a ship or a vase, and also called a tabernacle, as if the life growing in her was her congregation, as though she was a great sacred structure. But the embryonic Jesus didn't sit in church; he swam in the amniotic waters of his mother's womb; he was at sea because we are all sea creatures before we are land animals, and perhaps we all yearn for this dark ocean before we knew separation, perhaps it's an orientation before memory. He was in liquid and then a dry country, but at the river Jordan his cousin John baptized him, a rite defined as marking entry into the church. It says everything that you go into the water to go into the church that is also the mother who is originally the ocean.

When the scuttling animals who would eventually generate mammals who would eventually generate our species emerged from the ocean, I read recently, we had to become canteens that carried water with us, and the word "canteen" seemed striking. We land animals are constantly pouring liquids into our bodies that are bodies of water contained in the tiny flasks called cells, a word also used for the locked rooms prisoners are thrust into, and by the sack of skin. We are water walking toward the next drink. Water washes in again to cleanse, so water baptizes us, perhaps every time we come in contact with it, baptized by this glass of water on a summer day, by this shower, by this dishwashing, by this rain, by this swim, but baptized not in that purity that seeks to separate but that immersion against separation, against loneliness. Water is a temple, all this says.

So, there is a man with a beloved mother in his past and an ocean in his future and a great deal of clarity about his priorities. May he thrive and be exalted by the spacious beauty of the sea, may he come to the Pacific and look from the sandy edge onto this body of water that covers two-fifths of the Earth, may it give him some sense of the freedom of untrammeled space, may his imagination be carried on pelicans' wings, may it reach to the horizon of a clear day, may he walk on the clouds reflected on the wet sand of low tide, may he inhale the salt that is the salinity of the sea that is also the salinity of our blood and our tears.

Postscript: A year after Kevin Strickland's release, a local television report on station KSBH showed him wading in the sea, improving his health, spending time with family, and driving a car through open landscapes.

Credo

11 PM, NOVEMBER 5, 2024

They want you to feel powerless and to surrender and to let them trample everything and you are not going to let them. You are not giving up, and neither am I. The fact that we cannot save everything does not mean we cannot save anything and everything we can save is worth saving. You may need to grieve or scream or take time off, but you have a role no matter what, and right now good friends and good principles are worth gathering in. Remember what you love. Remember what loves you. Remember in this tide of hate what love is. The pain you feel is because of what you love.

The Wobblies used to say don't mourn, organize, but you can do both at once. You can be heartbroken or furious or both at once; you can scream in your car or on a cliff; you can also get up tomorrow and water the flowerpots and call someone who's upset and check your equipment for going onward. A lot of us are going to come under direct attack, and a lot of us are going to resist by building solidarity and sanctuary. Gather up your resources, the metaphysical ones that are heart and soul and care, as well as the practical ones.

People kept the faith in the dictatorships of South and Central America in the 1970s and 1980s, in the East Bloc countries and the

USSR, women are protesting right now in Iran and people there are writing poetry. There is no alternative to persevering, and that does not require you to feel good. You can keep walking whether it's sunny or raining. Take care of yourself and remember that taking care of something else is an important part of taking care of yourself, because you are interwoven with the ten trillion things in this single garment of destiny that has been stained and torn, but is still being woven and mended and washed.

Acknowledgments

No one has been more kind, more devoted, more encouraging, and more protective of my writing and me as a writer than my beloved literary agent, Frances Coady of Aragi, so my first thanks here are to her. Haymarket Books has been a haven for me for more than a decade now, and Anthony Arnove, copy editor Caroline Luft, publicity maven Jim Plank, and designer Rachel Cohen are generous, infinitely trustworthy, and ridiculously good at what they do. Being at a press driven by progressive ideals and publishing heroes of mine from Mariame Kaba to Angela Davis has been another blessing of being with this house. In the UK, this book will be published by Granta, where editor Bella Lacy and publicist Pru Rowlandson have been a joy to work with over the course of many projects. Thanks, too, to the foreign publishers who bring this work into the wider world.

And while the process of turning the essays I wrote at home into a piece in a periodical is often rendered invisible, I have benefited greatly from good and supportive editors in many publications, especially Amana Fontanella-Khan and Oliver Milman at the *Guardian* and Jonny Diamond at LitHub (where I was first brought by John Freeman when he was coeditor of that online journal). These are where the majority of essays in this book were first published, and I've been grateful to have these outlets whose views align so well with mine or at least give me room for what I think and believe (while the struggle for one's voice—in both style and ideological substance—to survive in the major East Coast publications is mostly, some of my writer friends and I have concluded, not worth it).

Thank you to all the often invisible people who edit, copyedit, design, print, and distribute my work, and to all the independent booksellers who support it when it appears in this form. Behind them all are readers; I am endlessly grateful (and still a little startled) that enough people want to read what I write that it's been the main way I've made my living for more than a third of a century. I am a writer because I am a reader, and readers share a faith in books—in the practice of quieting down and going deep, in the power of accurate description, in the passion to understand what the meanings and possibilities this life offers us are.

These years in which the essays were written have been full of wonder and horror, and I'm grateful to the people with whom I've faced both. In my climate community, the board (on which I'm honored to serve) and staff of Oil Change International, especially Red Constantino and Elizabeth Bast; the team at Third Act (on whose board I also serve), particularly Bill McKibben, Anna Goldstein, and my longtime friend and hero B Fulkerson; the tough and inspiring leaders at the Sunrise Movement; and a whole bunch of visionaries and heroes here and there and everywhere, including Terry Tempest Williams and Blake Spalding in Utah and Tzeporah Berman in British Columbia and Conchita Lozano Batista right across town from me and Thelma Young Lutunatabua in Fiji. The Auntie Sewing Squad was the best thing that happened to me during the pandemic, and more thanks and love to all the aunties and our founder Kristina Wong.

The biggest joys in my life remain the youngest people I love, the people I think of as I do my climate work, the people who may well be around for the beginning of the twenty-second century, so, thank you Maya, Ella, Atlas, Martin, Isaac, and Solomon, once again. Don't let anyone steal your joy.

This is the sixth book in a series that started in 2014 with *Men Explain Things to Me*, which Abby Weintraub designed so brilliantly that a bunch of other books soon came out with the same general big-white-letters-flush-left-against-a-solid-background format. By the time a few more essay anthologies had received the same design treatment, I realized that we were well on our way to making a rainbow in what I am amused to think of as the world's slowest gesture of queer solidarity; this yellow book follows red, orange, green, blue, and violet books. I like to think of *Hope in the Dark* with its black cover as the night that preceeded this diurnal rainbow.

Publication Credits

The essays in this book appeared in the following publications, sometimes in somewhat different versions and often under different titles:

The Agam Agenda, a climate/culture project of the Institute for Climate and Sustainable Cities, published *Harvest Moon: Poems and Stories from the Edge of the Climate Crisis* (2021) for which "Sky Full of Forests" served as an afterword.

The *Guardian* published "A Truce with the Trees," "Tortoise at the Mayfly Party," "Against Centrism and Its Biases," "Abortion Is an Economic Issue," "Feminism Has Just Begun," "Deep Time Versus Short Term," and "The Great Transformation."

The online journal Literary Hub published "On Letting Go of Certainty in a Story That Never Ends," "In Praise of the Meander," "On Not Meeting Nazis Halfway," "Masculinity as Radical Selfishness," "The Storykiller and His Sentence," and "Hope on Far Horizons."

The *London Review of Books* published "In the Shadow of Silicon Valley."

The *New York Times* published "Toward a Democracy of Voices" as "The Harvey Weinstein Verdict Is a Watershed—and a Warning."

The *Washington Post* published "Climate of Abundance."

The University of California Press published *The Auntie Sewing Squad Guide to Mask Making, Radical Care, and Racial Justice* (2022), which included "Insurrectionary Aunthood."